Gardeners' World

CAROL KLEIN

FLOWERS
Nature's Own to
Garden Grown

WITH PHOTOGRAPHS BY JONATHAN BUCKLEY

BOOKS

10 9 8 7 6 5 4 3 2 1

This book is published to accompany the television series entitled *Gardeners' World*, broadcast on BBC2 in 2013

Executive producer: Gill Tierney
Series producer: Liz Rumbold
Director: Tom Weston
Researcher: Rob Yeoman

Published in 2013 by BBC Books, an imprint of Ebury Publishing
A Random House Group company

Text © Carol Klein 2013
Photography © Jonathan Buckley 2013

Carol Klein has asserted her right to be identified as the author of this Work in accordance with the Copyright, Designs and Patents Act 1988

The Random House Group Limited Reg. 954009

Addresses for companies within the Random House Group can be found at www.randomhouse.co.uk

A CIP catalogue record for this book is available from the British Library

ISBN 978 1 84 990584 8

The Random House Group Limited supports The Forest Stewardship Council® (FSC®), the leading international forest certification organisation. Our books carrying the FSC label and printed on FSC® certified paper. FSC is the only forest certification scheme endorsed by leading environmental organisations, including Greenpeace. Our paper procurement policy can be found at www.randomhouse.co.uk

MIX
Paper from responsible sources
FSC® C015829

Commissioning editor: Lorna Russell
Project editor: Joe Cottington
Copy editor: Kevin Smith
Designer: Andrew Barron
Photographer: Jonathan Buckley

Colour origination by AltaImage, London
Printed and bound by Firmengruppe APPL, aprinta druck, Wemding, Germany

To buy books by your favourite authors and register for offers, visit www.randomhouse.co.uk

Contents

Introduction

There weren't many wild flowers in my childhood, but that just meant that those I met were all the more precious and memorable.

There were snowdrops, not from the edges of the A6, Manchester Road, but from deepest, darkest Cornwall. One of my grandma's sisters lived there and each year would send my grandma a bunch. The ritual when they arrived is one of my strongest memories. Me, my brothers and our cousins were summoned. When we were gathered together in the glass lean-to at the back of the house in Holly Avenue, my grandma would break the sealing wax, cut the string, fold back the thick brown paper and open the box within. There were the pristine white flowers, single snowdrops, their stems wrapped in lush moss, soft and brilliant green. Before you looked and marvelled, your nose took in the honeyed perfume, mingled with the smell of the ancient earth. Have you noticed how people always close their eyes when they are smelling something?

Another highlight was collecting armfulls of bluebells from Oak Wood, the one little patch of woodland left where we lived, with the tracks of the trains that carried coal from Sandhole colliery on its outskirts. They were always at their best when the youngest beech leaves first unfurled and both were gathered greedily, the only problem being how to carry them safely home to my mum when I had to grasp the handlebars of my bike. I was good at riding with one hand, anyway – or with no hands, come to that.

Once upon a time, wild flowers were part of everyone's life, not only in a Wordsworthian way, but more fundamentally. They were an integral part of the everyday poesy of life, the basis of folklore and legend, of magic and superstition. On a more visceral level they were food for man and beast, and the source of almost all medicine. Still, today, more than seventy per cent of our medicines are derived from plants.

Our connection with the wild flowers and plants that were once at the core of life has been worn thinner and thinner. From the enclosure of common land to the full-blown industrialization and urbanization of our environment and the onslaught of post-war monoculture farming with its dependence on chemicals, wild flowers have suffered badly.

ABOVE
Silene dioica. The red campion typifies the simple perfection of wild flowers.

OPPOSITE
Campion, cow parsley and buttercups disporting themselves along the road verge close to Glebe Cottage.

The experience of meeting wild flowers and learning about them deepens our knowledge, understanding and appreciation of the world. How can we expect our children to care for their planet if they have no connection with their own wild landscape and the plants that inhabit it?

As gardeners, the more we know about the plants under our care, the better we will treat them and the better they will repay us. So many of the plants we grow are somebody's wild flowers somewhere. When I started selling plants more than thirty years ago, I was seldom asked about a plant's provenance nor what it liked nor how it grew. Of course I told people anyway, as far as I knew. Now people want to know, they are keen to discover, from whatever source, that *Geranium psilostemon* was once called *Geranium armenum*, that where it comes from – in Armenia – it grows amongst scrubby grasses and other perennial plants. They know then that this little thing they buy from the garden centre in a small pot with a highly coloured plastic label, much bigger than the plant itself, describing its height and spread, with a symbol to indicate whether or not it prefers sun, has the potential to grow into a huge, virile clump of a plant, smothered in

magenta flowers with coal-black eyes. It will feed a thousand bees, throw its seed around and live for decades – indefinitely, if it is looked after, divided and nurtured. Its progeny may find their way to other gardens to enchant other families.

Our television strand and this book seek to look at some of our most seductive wild flowers and, side-by-side, find out about their cultivated cousins, the plants we know and love in our own gardens. It has been a huge delight to see these wildlings in their own homes, to feel the springy turf under your feet and kneel down on it to examine the intricacies of a harebell – pleated buds, hair-fine stems and fairy-hat bells. To come face-to-face with *Geranium sanguineum* var. *striatum* (which I shall always call *lancastriense*) on the sand dunes of Walney Island was a dream come true and an experience that will stay with me forever. Didn't even notice the force nine gale.

These meetings with wild flowers are seminal to my understanding of the place of plants in the world, and to my own very limited gardening knowledge. Anyone can do the same, kneel amongst them, feel the same thrill, touch the same petals. Most of us do that anyway.

Gardening is the most direct route to an understanding of what is important, to connect directly with the earth. It is a privilege and a pleasure and one that everyone should have the opportunity to join in.

This is just an introduction but already it feels as though the introduction could become a book. Instead I've written another book that follows on the next pages. I hope you enjoy it.

SPRING SHOOTS

Spring is surely the most exciting season. The gardener's pulse begins to race as they anticipate the arrival of the season that sets the year on its way. Any suspicion of green, any nuance of a flower, is welcomed, embraced, applauded.

The beech trees I can see from the window as I write this are leafless for a full six months. We may have enjoyed everything that has gone before, but now we need an injection of green and, whilst at first it may come as a dribble, pretty soon it becomes a torrent. The dark earth, seemingly barren for so long, yields the first fresh shoots and the buds of flowers.

The earth turns over in its sleep, stretches and wakes. Once started there is no stopping it. It is so humbling to feel yourself carried along with the surge, knowing this huge, inexorable force is in full and complete command, and submitting yourself to its power.

As I walk the dogs in late February and early March I'm constantly on the lookout for the first primrose. You search for the first sign of a pale bud, willing it to open and then, one day, there is a flower, and another, and another. Within weeks the lanes are lined with them and on sunny days their familiar scent fills your nostrils again.

So many of our spring plants are woodlanders, Cinderella plants that get the whole business done before the trees come into leaf. As the earth begins to warm, the bare branches that we wish into life provide the ideal conditions for primroses, wood anemones and violets to burst into growth, and the dun earth sparkles with tiny splashes of iridescent colour. Pulmonarias twinkle, the verdant star shoots of bluebells thrust their way through leaf litter and amongst the collapsed fronds of bracken. The overriding sepia gives way to spring as it creeps in, throwing its gentle green mantle over every hedgerow and woodland floor.

The flowers of bluebells will take their time, but in our gardens their relatives make an early entrance. Scillas, chianodoxa and muscari add blue to the springtime mix and the first fritillaries join them. Daffodils begin to appear. Before you know it there are sheets of yellow and white, accompanied by the brilliance of euphorbias. The first fern fronds stretch and unfurl. Polypody and asplenium have graced the woodland floor and the garden all winter long and though they, too, have new, fresh growth, it is their deciduous cousins that manifest the full upsurge of spring.

The earth breathes deeper and faster now. Spring has arrived.

Primroses

To call a flower the epitome of spring may seem a bit of a cliché, but in the case of the primrose, *Primula vulgaris*, it is perfectly apt. No other plant gives the same feeling of spring's inexorable progress – perfect, pale-lemon flowers with an egg-yolk centre balanced on slender stems as nude and pink as a baby bird. Rosettes of crinkled, fresh-green leaves sit comfortably in hedgerow or ditch, or smother the ground at the woodland's edge. It is the 'prima rosa' – the first flower of spring.

The primrose is the county flower of Devon, but there must be many people throughout the country who feel such an attachment to this joyous little flower, that they consider it is particularly special to their area and to them – their own primrose. Essentially an edge-of-woodland plant, along with man it has moved out to the banks and ditches he has created. Where I live in the Devon countryside, hedgerows are alive with its pallid flowers and, on a sunny day, the air is filled with their sweet scent – available just where it is needed – at nose level. In its natural habitat it seeds itself around, each new plant becoming an established clump, spreading itself out gradually in search of nutrients amongst the debris of leaves and moss.

It has always been picked – little bunches of it, tied with soft wool and presented as gifts or love tokens. It has special associations with Easter. Unlike so many of our native flowers, resilient primroses seem to be adaptable to man's encroachment. Nowadays more of us get to enjoy their sunny presence, even if it is in our own gardens or on motorway embankments as we hurtle by.

Cultivated cousins

No doubt, wild primroses have found their way into gardens from the very first time plots were set aside to cultivate food, and though they can be eaten and drunk (primrose wine must be a delicacy), it is for the joy they bring to spirit and soul that they are prized. They and their offspring are celebrated in *Gerard's Herbal*, published in 1597, and for centuries people have cherished both the wild primrose and its multifarious cultivars.

One of the oldest of these, *Primula* 'Wanda', has been a popular plant for decades, possibly centuries. Its strident magenta flowers are a familiar feature to town and country dwellers alike. It was the first primula I ever saw. When I was little it used to fill the tiny front gardens of the miners' and millworkers' terraces, sometimes travelling right up the street. It is an easy plant to 'pass around' and, since it is almost indestructible, it offers encouragement to new gardeners. Recently it has lent its genes to a whole range of 'Wanda' hybrids – short, stocky plants often with dark leaves and richly coloured dark flowers with little yellow in their centres, an inheritance from another contributor, *Primula* Cowichan Group.

OPPOSITE
Devon banks are the perfect venue to both see and smell primroses. Their perfume, especially on a warm day at the start of spring, is honeyed, best enjoyed with eyes closed.

At Glebe Cottage we grow a version of this we call P. 'Black Magic'.

The Cowichan Group was developed by Florence Bellis, an American concert pianist who, having no work at the time of the Great Depression, decided to earn her living breeding primulas and trying to sell them. She settled as a 'haylofter' in a barn in Oregon with two pianos, a tattered trunk and called her house, and her new enterprise, Barnhaven. Originally all her seed was from England and over a period of more than thirty years she worked on perfecting different strains, including the Cowichans. P. Striped Victorians Group, P. Chartreuse Group, P. 'Desert Sunset' and P. Grand Canyon Group are examples of her work. Later, Florence succeeded in developing a seed strain that regularly produced double-flowered forms of the primrose. Using pollen from an exquisite old French primrose, P. 'Marie Crousse', she crossed and back-crossed her plants. Double primroses are sterile, so it was no mean feat that after years of patient work she achieved her objective. Many of the modern double primroses owe their existence to her perseverance.

Cultivars such as P. 'Miss Indigo', with its navy blue flowers touched with white, or P. 'Dawn Ansell', a pure, gleaming white jack-in-the-green, its many petals encased in white calyces, are probably descended from Barnhaven primulas. Modern doubles are often micro-propagated in their thousands nowadays. Some still retain some of the grace of old varieties like P. vulgaris 'Lilacina Plena' and P. vulgaris 'Alba Plena', although others are decidedly dumpy. Because double flowers cannot set seed, their flowers tend to last a long time, which makes them a particularly attractive proposition in the garden. Their cultivation is exactly the same as that for single primroses.

Two other strains in which Florence Bellis took particular interest were the gold-laced polyanthus beloved by the old 'florists' who grew them for competition, and the 'Elizabethan' primroses, all manner of bizarre polyanthus and primroses with extended calyces or one flower inside another. This last group is named after types of Elizabethan hosiery (hose-in-hose and pantaloons).

P. Gold-laced Group has flowers like black velvet with each petal ringed in bright yellow. The flowers are held symmetrically at the top of a straight stem. Together with the precisely gold-edged petals this creates a very formal impression.

This quest for perfection was ridiculed by the 'natural gardening' fraternity – William Robinson, Gertrude Jekyll and Ellen Willmott all poured scorn on the artificiality of this pursuit. Nowadays, along with auriculas, these intriguing flowers find favour with many gardeners who love the quirky and the whimsical.

OPPOSITE TOP LEFT
Polyanthus 'Black Magic' with petals like dark, rich velvet.
TOP RIGHT
Later on the peony's leaves will provide shade for the dwindling primroses. Right now they make a perfect partnership.
OPPOSITE BELOW
Primula 'Silver Lace'. Sometimes these old-fashioned flowers are edged in silver, sometimes in gold.

There are a host of primroses from which to choose, whatever your taste. Most of us would love *P.* 'Guinevere', a dark-leaved beauty with pale, lilac-pink flowers. It is immensely useful amongst early spring bulbs. *P.* 'Blue Riband' is even more ground-hugging, with vivid-blue petals rimmed with crimson. These are both true primroses bearing one flower on a single stem. Some of the dainty-named polyanthus, their flowers clustered on top of the stems, are just as desirable. *P.* 'Lady Greer' is one of the most understated. It is a charming old polyanthus variety with dainty, pale-cream, slightly belled flowers.

Most primulas look best in a naturalistic setting but they can be used formally too. Try *P. vulgaris* with pushkinia, scillas or chinodoxa and *Anemone nemorosa*, our native wood anemone. *P.* Gold-laced Group and *Ophiopogon planiscapus* 'Nigrescens' make a cutting-edge combination in a shady container, perhaps with the silver spikes of *Astelia chathamica* as a centrepiece.

P. 'Black Magic' works under the crimson-backed leaves of *Rheum* 'Ace of Hearts' with red-eyed *Euphorbia* × *martinii* in the background. Plant a drift of *P.* 'Blue Riband', *P.* 'Tawny Port' or any of the purply-bronze-leaved hybrids amongst dark hellebores and blue pulmonarias.

Primroses are incredibly tough and will flourish in a garden situation providing they get what they need. They thrive in soil that is on the damp side, preferably humus-rich, and with adequate shade during the hottest part of the year.

They love to be divided fairly frequently, the old, hard, rhizomatous roots discarded. The new pieces from the outside of the clump should have their white roots trimmed back to about 10cm (4in), the length of your palm. They don't get this sort of treatment in the hedgerow, but there they are able to spread outwards from their old crown and make fresh roots or to seed themselves about. The same method can be practised to keep most cultivated descendants of *Primula vulgaris*, and its close alpine cousin, *Primula juliae*, in vigorous growth indefinitely. There are numerous hybrids and cultivars of these European species in cultivation, and from these plants the hordes of highly-coloured polyanthus and primroses that throng garden-centre shelves have been developed.

Primroses are hedgerow plants and enjoy dappled shade. Areas under deciduous trees or between shrubs suit them well. Alternatively they can be planted between clumps of herbaceous perennials which, although they will be barely visible when the primroses are at their peak, will provide shade at the height of the summer when the primroses are resting.

When planting, work in plenty of organic matter – compost or leaf mould. Ensure the crown of the plant is level with the soil. Firm in well. Water thoroughly and mulch with compost, rotted muck or bark. And don't forget your plants after flowering – apply an organic liquid feed and water well in dry weather.

OPPOSITE
Gertrude Jekyll described the perfect time to divide primulas as being 'when the flowers are on the wain'.

Wood anemones

Close to where we live in North Devon is an ancient wood. There are some large oak trees, but most of it is hazel. Long ago it would have been coppiced regularly. Now the hazels touch overhead and in summer woodbine, our native honeysuckle, creates an extra canopy. Underfoot, plush moss softens the contours climbing up trunks and smothering fallen branches.

Often in early spring there is the smell of deer, later ramsons (wild garlic) carpets the margins of the wood spilling down its steep slope. Bluebells permeate its shady depths, spreading their blue haze indefinitely. Before bluebells and garlic think of emerging the ground is bare. Walk past on a gloomy day in early April and leaf litter and moss are all you see. On dull days wood anemones hang their heads, petals furled tightly to protect precious pollen. But the next day, when the sun shines from a clear spring sky, suddenly the woodland floor is transformed as if by a magic wand. Countless white flowers hold their heads aloft, petals outstretched to the warmth and light – they follow the sun's passage from east to west offering up sweet nectar to itinerant insects.

Anemone nemorosa, the wood anemone, is one of our most beloved wild flowers, occurring widely all over the British Isles in woodland and shady hedgerow. In early spring it pushes up wiry stems supporting lacy leaves wrapped around its infant buds. Its petals or sepals are dusty pink on the outside; inside they are pure and pristine white. Though there are more than forty selections of wood anemone listed, none surpasses the simple beauty of the species.

Cultivated cousins

Nobody hybridises wood anemones, but sharp-eyed botanists and gardeners have spotted variations in the wild and had the presence of mind to make them available. Some are exquisite, others bizarre. Some have been chosen for the size of their flowers, others for their colour, yet others for some quirky characteristic.

An anemone with no sepals seems like a contradiction in terms, yet *A. nemorosa* 'Virescens' is just that. Mounds of cut, lacy foliage support flowers completely composed of lacy bracts. It is one of the most textural plants in the garden and a perfect contrast to the large bold leaves of trilliums, early hostas and hellebores. Subtle and understated but the sort of plant that enriches a woodland scheme.

Another restrained wood anemone is *A. nemorosa* 'Bracteata Pleniflora'. As its title suggests it is a combination of sepals and bracts, all deliciously interspersed to make one of the prettiest of these woodland cinderellas. Every flower is different from the next, with varying amounts of green and white in each flowerhead. In 'Green Fingers' there is a boss of green petaloid bracts inside a circlet of white sepals. White spring flowers tinged with green are always attractive, but these two anemones are fascinating as well.

No wood anemone could be accused of

OPPOSITE
Alongside the moat at
Great Dixter, primroses,
wood anemones and
buttercups carpet the path.

being flamboyant but one, *A. nemorosa* 'Vestal', is always eye-catching. Without doubt this is the crème de la crème since there is hardly a flower anywhere to compare with the immaculate whiteness of her flowers. A ring of flat petals supports a cascade of slender petalloid bracts. In common with so many double flowers, 'Vestal' is sterile, no seed is produced and the flowers continue to look pristine for weeks, unlike single-flowered varieties whose petals fall soon after pollination. 'Alba Plena' is similar, but its central petals are longer, losing some of the perfect balance of 'Vestal'. If you need big, pure-white flowers then go for 'Leeds Variety' – it's simple and impactful.

Blue is one of the colours of spring and there are several named blue-flowered anemonies, each one of which is claimed by its devotees to be the best. *A. nemorosa* 'Blue Bonnet' is neat and dark, 'Royal Blue' is taller. There is 'Atrocaerulea', which is the deepest blue, and whilst 'Bowles Purple' has a deep violet reverse, its interior is definitely blue.

For me the most beguiling selections are those whose blue flowers verge on the grey. In *A. nemorosa* 'Robinsoniana' the inside of the sepals is pure azure blue with a boss of golden stamens, but the reverse is the colour of a wood pigeon's breast. The flowers are lax and elegant when closed; when they are full open they just draw you in. Another ethereal silvery blue-flowered selection is 'Allenii'. If anything it is even more grey than 'Robinsoniana'. Both are substantial enough to draw attention to themselves but wistful enough to look at one with the rest of spring's entourage. They mingle perfectly with wan primroses, and are equally at home offsetting the blazing stars of *Caltha palustris* (marsh marigold) or celandines.

When we moved here a clump of wood anemones growing along one of the hedges was decidedly pink. It has been divided and distributed to different parts of the garden, although we usually try to restrict ourselves to one variety per bed – our shady garden is sub-divided into smaller areas. These pink forms must appear from time to time in nature. On one broad, shady road verge close to us the whole bank is teeming with white wood anemones, but through the centre of the colony is a broad swathe of a pink form, as though someone had taken a huge brush loaded with watery pink paint and splashed it on liberally. *A. nemorosa* 'Cedric's Pink' and 'Lismore Pink' are named forms, and 'Bill Baker's Pink', named after the brilliant plant hunter, is supposed to be one of the best.

To make more, lift them carefully in late summer, break into chunks, each with a resting bud and a few fibrous roots, and replant them an inch or two deep adding fresh leaf-mould. Take care, though, they can become addictive.

Lungworts

Few wild flowers are ostentatious, but there are some that seem particularly shy – plants of a retiring nature who only reveal themselves hesitantly. The wild Lungworts, *Pulmonaria longifolia* and *P. officinalis*, are prime examples. Members of the borage family, they exhibit the usual ratio within that clan of flower-to-foliage volume – about one to 10, but their bright little flowers, in shades of red and blue (often both at the same time), are treasured early in the year. In common with other borages, their blue flowers often change to pink as they fade, giving rise to several country names – Joseph and Mary and Soldiers and Sailors amongst them.

The Doctrine of Signatures was the medieval practice where plants were used to treat ailments of the organs they looked like. Under it, *P. officinalis* was given its common name of Lungwort by apothecaries, struck by similarities between its leaves and lungs, and henceforth used to treat respiratory disease. *P. longifolia* is a plant of the downs, the New Forest and the Isle of Wight. It wasn't an easy task to find it growing wild, it has almost disappeared, but our researcher, Rob, found wonderful examples close to the Solent in damp meadowland at Exbury Gardens. It was early in the year, and clumps with small, bright flowers spangled the grass. At first it was barely visible, but the closer you looked, the more you could see. Its colonies spread over the whole area, the majority hugging the ground close to the gullies and little streams that criss-crossed the meadow.

Most perennial plants use winter as an opportunity to hibernate, gathering their strength underground to produce the shoots and flowers of the new season. There are only a few exceptions, and for gardeners they provide a continuum between the old season and the new. To reach their peak at this time of year, plants need to be robust – toughing it out through rain, snow and frost demands a strong constitution. Pulmonarias have rough, durable leaves perfectly adapted to winter weather. Their handsome foliage, bespangled with silver splodges and spots, sparkles amongst the winter mire. Easy to grow, they thrive even in the most unprepossessing places – in dark, dank corners and even in heavy, stodgy clay. They are must-have plants, in their glory during the first months of the year, and since their foliage

OPPOSITE
Pulmonarias are happy mingling. Here, *Pulmonaria* 'Blue Ensign' with cow parsley and anemones.

ABOVE
Pulmonaria 'Diana Clare' with typically 'changeable' flower colour.

is evergreen they go on to provide a useful background to later-flowering woodlanders or summer perennials.

Cultivated cousins

Selections of *P. officinalis* and *P. saccharata* offer flowers in a range of blues and reds. Some of the most appealing are those with pale blue flowers – *P.* Opal and *P. officinalis* 'Blue Mist' are two of the best, both lovely with snowdrops and dark or pale-green hellebores. *P.* 'Sissinghurst White' is a classic lungwort and looks apt wherever it is placed. All three have well-marked leaves and their foliage continues the show around campanulas or late-flowering anemones.

In some pulmonarias, the spots join up to create silver leaves. These can be heart-shaped as in *P.* 'Majesté', or narrow and linear as in *P.* 'Cotton Cool' which Hazel Bishop showed us on *Gardeners' World* in her garden of the same name, where she found it.

A Dutch selection, *P. longifolia* 'Ankum', has long, narrow and silvery leaves with a smart, dark-green edge. Young leaves are heavily spotted with silver and eventually all the spots join up so that the whole leaf surface becomes iridescent. A collection of these plants in winter looks like a colony of silver starfish.

Some have no spots at all. *P. angustifolia*, a native species, has plain leaves accompanied by brilliant-blue flowers. A sport from this, *P.* 'Blue Ensign', has large royal-blue flowers set amongst very dark, red-backed leaves – outstanding. It is far and away the best blue pulmonaria of the lot, with the largest, richest flowers of any. It is a superb plant, reliable and long-flowering, and to see it accompanying big clumps of dark hellebores with a sprinkling of snowdrops can easily change minds and turn late winter into your favourite season.

Often the first lungwort to flower, *P. rubra*, cheers up the most dismal reaches of the garden with its light-green leaves and coral-coloured flowers. It is an 'obvious' plant – some would describe it as coarse, but it is jolly and dependable, often flowering before Christmas (one of its country names is Christmas Cowslip) and going on until March. *P. rubra* 'David Ward' is a version discovered by, and named after, the head of Beth Chatto's nursery. Its leaves have broad cream margins, which helps them stand out well in shady places. Since it scorches when grown in full sun, make a virtue of necessity by using it in dark corners.

All pulmonarias are easy to cultivate given plenty of humus in the soil and dappled shade – they don't need a perfect woodland floor to prove their worth. Because they are so strong and willing, they are ideal candidates for all those awkward dingy corners in town and city gardens where nothing seems to want to grow. Planted with extra organic matter, old muck or a handful or two of your best home-

OPPOSITE TOP LEFT
The best blue, *Pulmonaria* 'Blue Ensign'.
TOP RIGHT
Silver and green, the painted fern *Athyrium niponicum* var. *pictum* with

a silver-splodged lungwort.
OPPOSITE BELOW
Red-flowered lungworts with spotted leaves are few and far between. *P.* 'Hazel Kaye's Red' is one of the best.

remains uppermost. Providing the cuttings are lined up alongside one another, and promptly pushed into compost, it is easy. Cuttings should be between 2.5cm (1in) and 5cm (2in) long depending on their volume – the skinnier the cutting, the longer it needs be. Dibble them into the compost so that the top is flush with the surrounding compost. Cover with a layer of grit and water well. They can be pushed into gritty, free-draining compost in pots or deep seed trays, or one at a time in cell trays or modules, which means less root disturbance when they are potted on later.

For other lungworts that can't be reproduced from root cuttings, the answer is simply to divide your plants. Dig up the whole clump, discard old, woody centres and replant fresh young pieces. Keep the fresh, young pieces around the edge of the clump, which should have a well-developed root system. Ground should be improved before replanting with copious amounts of home-made compost or leaf-mould. Although pulmonarias can manage even in heavy clay soils, when any plant is divided and replanted it will get off to a much more rapid start if the soil is friable.

made compost, they should settle down well and flourish, needing little attention for years. They are some of the most laid-back plants around, rewarding the minimum of effort with a splendid display just when it's needed most.

Sometimes pulmonarias will seed themselves, and though some of the seedlings can be special, growing from seed is not a reliable way of increasing your plants. There are two methods of propagating lungworts – both are vegetative so you are producing clones (exact copies of the parent plant). The first is from root cuttings – this is a good method for increasing numbers of *P. longifolia* (of which there are many different cultivars and selections) and for some hybrids such as *P.* 'Moonstone'. You can harvest material either by digging up the whole plant or by carefully severing a few roots while the plant stays in the soil. A quick burrow down should reveal some suitable material.

Polarity is all-important, making sure the end closest to the crown of the plant always

OPPOSITE
Pieces are replanted in groups with added leaf-mould or compost.
ABOVE
Pulling apart your pulmonaria plants every two or three years re-invigorates them. Top foliage is trimmed back.

Daffodils

Which plant best personifies spring? For optimists it is the snowdrop, for realists the primrose, but for most it must be the daffodil. Nothing says spring so categorically. There may be frosts after its arrival, but by the time the familiar yellow trumpets start to sound, the wheels of the year have begun to grind inexorably forward.

Narcissus pseudonarcissus is our native daffodil. It is small, strong and stocky. The flowers emerge from a papery spathe, gently turning themselves downwards to protect pollen and to shelter obliging insects inside their deep, yellow trumpets. The outer perianth is pale soft yellow. These are Wordsworth's host, the Lent lily.

Anyone coming across them cannot help smiling, and that is after the initial gasp of total delight. Close to where we live in North Devon, the banks of the local rivers are gilded with hundreds of their small but brilliant-yellow flowers. They relish the heavy soil and seem to enjoy the few weeks they spend practically submerged. No doubt when the water returns to its usual level, it leaves behind all manner of minerals and nutrients. Many bulbs would object to inundation, but these little daffodils have evolved with the constant rise and fall of the water and get better year on year.

Not so long ago the dancing yellow flowers of *N. pseudonarcissus* could be seen displaying themselves in woodland and along river banks up and down the country. Many of its former homes have disappeared, subsumed by development and drainage. To add insult to injury, just as with the snowdrop, unthinking people helped themselves and colonies dwindled or were destroyed. But those were the bad old days. Nowadays we are more aware of how populations of plants can be decimated by human action. Thankfully, conservation is higher on the agenda.

Where it has been left undisturbed *N. pseudonarcissus* increases well, seeding itself around, making vast sheets of yellow. Most often it grows in grass. This is by far the best way to see most daffodils. Not only does the grass provide the perfect foil for the yellow of the flowers, but it hides their demise and offers shade when old flowers and dying foliage shrivel. Often seed has been set at this stage, and the growing grass must shelter the tiny shoots that gradually emerge after the swollen seedhead sinks to the ground.

Equally, in a garden situation narcissi are at their best growing in grass, and the more informal and meadowy it is the better. Bulbs and clipped grass just don't go together – their needs are diametrically different. Bulbs need to be left to reabsorb all the goodness from their foliage while manicured lawns need to be cut short frequently. Large drifts of *N. pseudonarcissus* planted in grass close to trees work best. In a meadow setting they can be planted alongside other bulbs, such as *Fritillaria meleagris* and

OPPOSITE
The pale trumpets of this dainty daffodil, *Narcissus* 'W. P. Milner', herald the spring.

camassia, and with a variety of suitable meadow perennials. Left to their own devices, they will have the opportunity to set and distribute seed.

The Lent lily is ideal for orchard planting too. Even when the 'orchard' consists of just one tree, groups of *N. pseudonarcissus* amongst its roots, and straying into the surrounding area, make a delightful picture. Beware planting a solid circle between the trunk and the circumference of the branches. Any symmetry in their arrangement mars the simple beauty of these wildlings.

Cultivated cousins

The Tenby daffodil, *N. obvallaris*, is another native, although this time in clear yellow. It is equally suited to the same informal treatment as *N. pseudonarcissus*, to which it is closely related.

The soft, milky-lemon colouring (just like lemon mousse) of *N.* 'W.P. Milner' is always easy to use. This is one of the most outstanding of all the small narcissi. Although a cultivar, it has the grace and simplicity of a wild daffodil. It was first listed by Peter Barr, the famous Covent Garden nurseryman, in his catalogue of 1884, so has stood the test of time well. It prefers damp soil and needs deep planting to prevent its bulbs splitting up and becoming unproductive. *N. moschatus*, from the Pyrenees, has similar 'moonlight' colouring and a quirky tendency to twist its outside petals.

There are several diminutive, wild, trumpet daffodils that are perfectly suited to growing through very short grass or even moss. The first, and the smallest at 8–10cm (3–4in) tall, is *N. asturiensis*, which sometimes starts to flower in February. It is often grown from seed and the colour can vary. If possible choose it in flower. *N. minor*, with a pale perianth and yellow trumpet, is only slightly taller. *N. minor* pumilus *ambig.* is taller again, standing a full 15cm (6in) tall. It has very dainty flowers of brilliant yellow.

All these trumpet daffodils bear their flowers singly. They make their impact by force of numbers rather than multiple flowers on each stem. Their colour is never garish. They fit in wonderfully around the edges of informal urban gardens, under hedges, fences and walls. In more rural settings they have the perfect persona for hedgerow planting, so much more fitting than the eye-wateringly garish clumps of vivid, large-flowered hybrids, which shock and disorientate those travelling along many a country road.

There are several old trumpet varieties that share the relaxed look with the wild species and are recommended for naturalising in longer grass. *N.* 'Golden Lady' has long trumpets held on 40cm (16in) stems and flowers early. *N.* 'Topolino' is sturdy and short with neat foliage.

OPPOSITE
We use this fragrant double jonquil all over the brick garden.
TOP LEFT
In black plastic pots.
TOP RIGHT
Later, in full bloom, the pots are lowered into galvanized buckets.

BELOW LEFT
Sometimes, for extra impact, we plant lots in a tree tub inside one of our lovely old coppers.
BELOW RIGHT
Occasionally they're planted direct into the ground, here with the first pristine shoots of *Iris pseudacorus* 'Variegata'.

Trumpet daffodils are perfectly happy in beds and borders where there is no grass. Planted where their dying foliage will not lower the tone, amongst herbaceous early-risers such as bold aquilegia or verdant hemerocallis, they can be left to their own devices. Hybrids should be deadheaded but species can be left to set and distribute seed.

N. 'W.P. Milner' looks even paler and more interesting alongside the large, beetroot-red leaves of *Bergenia cordifolia* 'Purpurea' or *B.* 'Ballawley Red'. Even if their rather puce flowers appear simultaneously with those of the daffodil, there should be no shock waves. At Glebe Cottage we have this endearing little daffodil amongst *Lysimachia ciliata* 'Firecracker' in a damp border with heavy soil.

Blue-flowered pulmonaria are perfect companions for the smaller narcissi, and the lungwort's mature leaves hide a multitude of sins. Both prefer heavy soil. *Pulmonaria* Opal or *P. officinalis* 'Blue Mist' make a quiet harmony with *Narcissus pseudonarcissus*. For something more invigorating, try *Pulmonaria* 'Blue Ensign' with the clear-yellow blooms of *Narcissus minor* 'Little Gem'.

When we filmed at Doddington Hall with Antony Jarvis, one of his major goals in the beautiful grounds there, bursting with both wild and cultivated narcissi, was to group the same kinds together to give more impact. To this end he digs up thousands of bulbs each year and transplants them. This is performed whilst they are in flower (the easiest time to recognise them), digging close to the bulbs in question

with a tree spade. He winkles them out, makes a deep slit in the grass in their new home, drops them in position and finishes off with a sturdy stamp. It works.

The majority of trumpet narcissi prefer damp, heavy ground. To supply extra nutrients on thin dry soils, a top dressing of good humus-rich compost can be worked in around their stems after flowering. This can still be done where they are growing in grass, although the grass will also benefit and grow more strongly.

When planting in grass, use a bulb planter, which will take out plugs of earth easily. I have an old one with a long handle, which is operated from a standing position. Take out the divot of earth and remove the top inch or two complete with grass roots. Invert this piece in the bottom of the new hole, push in the bulb firmly and supply it with a generous helping of planting mixture (preferably loamy potting soil with extra bonemeal). Replace the leftovers of the original soil.

Vary distances between the bulbs to ensure a random, natural look. Within a short space of time, big drifts can be created. This is an efficient way to plant or replant all narcissi. If planting in a bank or hedgerow, a small sharp trowel may be the best tool to use. Locate tree roots with a hand fork before attempting to excavate.

OPPOSITE
What better foil for *Narcissus* 'Thalia' than a carpet of woodruff.

Violets

On a country walk along hedge-bound lanes or skirting the edges of woods, the violet you are most likely to see is the dog violet. Its botanical name is *Viola riviniana*, but there are a number of other names for it (or species close to it) probably resulting from the fact that in nature it is very variable. It is quite likely to cross with other very similar species, too. 'Dog' is a prefix denoting that this is a plant lower down the pecking order than the one most celebrated – in this case *V. odorata*, the sweet violet.

We live in Devon, a county long associated with violets, and though Devon violets are almost certainly *V. odorata*, the violet that peeps out amongst grasses, primroses and the early shoots of wood-sage along Pixie Lane, our route to the nearest road, is the dog violet. Its lack of perfume is forgotten in the delight of seeing its flurry of pretty flowers making a purple haze (nothing could be further from Jimi Hendrix) amongst the vernal green. Some years there are lots of flowers, in others very few, even though

it is a perennial. It seeds freely and when it has little competition can colonise every available space.

When I was little, my dad used to take the family out on excursions on Sundays, partly to treat us but also to indulge in his favourite occupation – going as fast as possible in whatever fancy speedmobile he happened to have at that time (there were lots and he constantly changed them). One of the favourites, it was certainly mine, was a tomato-soup-red Austin Atlantic convertible, a car built secondarily for export to the USA, but primarily for speed. My mum and I, though we enjoyed the excitement just as much as the male contingent, had another agenda! A favourite destination for these trips – plausible from Manchester – was North Wales. As we hurtled along country roads the scenery changed until we were immersed in steep banks under the canopy of trees. In April the branches were bare but the ground beneath them was already bustling with spring's Cinderellas. 'Please can we stop, Dad, we need to spend a penny?' Out we'd tumble, crashing up the slope through old hazel coppice until we were out of sight and then we'd collapse in fits of giggles and squeals of delight into cushions of violets and carpets of primroses.

ABOVE
White violets sounds like a contradiction in terms but there is something extra-special about them. *Viola odorata* 'Albiflora' at Great Dixter.

OPPOSITE
The true sweet violet, *Viola odorata*, in all its charm.

Though there are wild populations still of *V. odorata*, they are few and far between and sometimes it's difficult to tell whether or not they are truly creatures of the wild or have made their way from nearby gardens. They are instantly distinguishable from dog violets. Their leaves are brighter green, bigger and softer too, and though there may be fewer flowers they too are more substantial. The most distinctive difference, though, is their perfume.

Out of the hedgerows and into the open field, other violets hold sway. Chief amongst them is the little annual field pansy, *V. arvensis*, a plant apparently on the increase since modern farming methods suit it well. It is close to, and often crosses with, the wild pansy, *V. tricolor*.

Violas and wild pansies have 'faces' alluded to in many of their country names, often having streaks, lines and areas of sharply delineated colour, which presumably look like whiskers or hair, eyes or noses. Cat's face is one such name, though the name that my mum and grandma used was heartsease. My daughters too know it by this name, and we are lucky enough to see it off and on, especially in one field close by which has now won organic status.

Violets and violas have evolved with specialised environments, adapting themselves to specific conditions. When we visited Walney Island off the Cumbrian coast for the programme, and again when Jonathan and I were adventuring on Braunton Burrows, we saw the pretty little dune pansy, a sub-species of *V. tricolor*, growing among Marram Grass in pure sand.

Cultivated cousins

Once upon a time there would have been bunches of sweet violets in the florists' shops and flower stalls in the spring. *V. odorata* is a native of the British Isles although it is more common in the south of the country. Often 'wild' populations are garden escapees – the sweet violet was often cultivated in cottage gardens. The Parma violet has an even more intense perfume, and its scent is just like the sweets, or '*cachoux*', which were once a popular confection. Although *V. odorata* is hardy it benefits from a warm, sheltered spot. Parma Violets need glass protection during the winter, especially if their flowers are to remain unsullied. *V.* 'Duchesse de Parme' is a famed double cultivar with an exotic scent, though *V.* 'Marie-Louise' is said to have the most powerful perfume.

V. 'Maggie Mott' is an old viola cultivar with exceptionally large flowers of pale lavender, darker at the edges. If you like your flowers in strange and interesting colours, *V.* 'Irish Molly' might be right up your street. The bizarre combination of brown and yellow is unique, although a seed strain, *V.* 'Green Goddess', produces variations on the same theme. All are useful and easy to combine with other plants, brilliant with smaller-flowered narcissi, especially yellow cultivars.

V. cornuta is the viola we use most at Glebe Cottage. Typically its flowers are a soft shade of lavender (some would call it blue). There are cultivars with deep-purple flowers, and there are two white forms, one smaller and more compact but both immensely useful. They make brilliant ground cover under old shrub roses and as edging plants in informal borders. They can be used also to create 'recesses' between taller plants without getting too gangly. Coping admirably with shade they also make pretty companions for spring woodlanders, and are excellent amongst taller, shady subjects such as ferns or Solomon's seal. Although *V. cornuta* has its main flowering in late spring, it continues to produce flowers on and off throughout the summer so may still be in bloom to partner late-flowering anemones or *Kirengeshoma palmata*.

When it is doing well, but getting a bit too effusive and there are more seedpods than flowers, it can be sheared to within a couple of inches of the ground or cut back with secateurs. When they are short and compact, these prunings can be used as cuttings. In fact, if you want to increase your stock you have the choice of three methods: cuttings, division or seed sowing. Cuttings work well and are easy to root. Select short stems, carefully removing the bottom leaves, and dibble into trays, pots or modules of gritty compost. Many cuttings benefit from having warm bottoms and being placed in a heated propagator, violas, on the other hand, root most easily in cool conditions – just place pots or trays of cuttings in a cold frame or a sheltered corner outdoors. When they start to make new growth, and there are signs of white roots pushing through the base of the pots, turn them out gently and pot individually. Alternatively, or perhaps additionally if you want a lot of plants, clumps can be pulled apart into pieces all with their own roots. Seed can also be sown – the seed capsules are delightful, split into three separate chambers with three rows of seed in each.

When grown under glass violets are sometimes prone to attack by red spider mite, but this is not a problem when grown outside. Being hedgerow dwellers they love leafy, humus-rich soil and some shade during the summer.

Many violas also have excellent perfume and, although they are later into flower when they start in April, their season goes on and on. Regular deadheading and an occasional liquid feed with an organic fertiliser should keep them in fine fettle.

OPPOSITE
Sitting in the spring sunshine. None of the violets at my feet was ever planted.

Spurge

We filmed our wild wood spurge, *Euphorbia amygdaloides*, on a big grassy verge alongside the road by the River Mole. Though we had hunted closer to Glebe Cottage for a suitable location, early and over-zealous verge- and hedge-cutting had decimated several populations remembered from previous years. Remembered vividly too, as the wood spurge creates splashes of flashing colour along our hedgerows. It often crops up with bluebells, or earlier on with self-seeded honesty escaped from a nearby garden – the combination of magenta-purple with lime green is worth copying. If the honesty heads are left intact they will stay all through the winter accompanying the hummocks of euphorbia, which often put on a fairly respectable show through till spring. *E. amygdaloides* grows at the woodland edge or amongst scrubby undergrowth at the base of hedges and in ditches. It is perennial and seeds freely, sometimes making large colonies.

Euphorbiaceae, the spurge family, is huge, though represented in temperate regions by a relatively small number of species. Even within this group there are species that thrive in almost every kind of situation in our gardens; some are low and scrambling and demand full sun and poor soil, others thrive on a lavish diet and need ample moisture at their roots. Some love shade, others are only happy when they are sunbaked.

Despite their creating such a vivid, retina-searing show, their flowers are tiny. It is the cyathium leaves (we used to call these bracts) rather than the flowers that make the impact. In most cases they are dramatic lime green, almost yellow, though occasionally, as in *E. griffithii* 'Fireglow', they may be vivid orange. No doubt this is an evolutionary development to attract insect pollinators. Unexpectedly, though the plant itself can have a slightly unpleasant smell, in most cases the flowers have a sweet perfume. Again this is probably an aid to pollination, needed because spurges flower early when there are few bees about. Heightened perfume surely shortens the odds.

All euphorbias produce a milky sap when their stems are broken or cut. This is an irritant and can burn the skin, especially in sunny weather. When pruning or cutting back euphorbia it is always advisable to wear gloves. Many of the plants in this family are poisonous, the most famous perhaps being ricinus – the castor-oil plant. While it is economically important as the source of castor oil, it has also been used as a weapon of torture and by terrorists as a biological or chemical weapon. Don't be put off, whatever its down side, *Ricinus communis* is one of the most exciting plants you can grow if you want to bring extra drama to a hot border, or find a centrepiece for a sensational container planting.

Start ricinus from seed sown any time from March onwards. The seeds are fascinating, and

OPPOSITE
Our wood spurge, *Euphorbia amygdaloides*, injects vivid splashes of lime green along road verges and at the woodland edge. Unforgettable.

look like hand-decorated beans. They're big, so sow them individually, either into separate pots or into modules giving each bean its own compartment. Once plants have made a decent root system and are a few inches high, pot them on and keep them moving into bigger pots. During late May or early June they are strong enough to take up their final positions in the open border, or standing out in really big pots to spend the summer adding glamour. Where they come from, ricinus can grow to tree-like proportions, though they are tender and cannot stand any frost. So here they must be treated as annuals, though that doesn't stop them making a tremendous impact while they last.

Cultivated cousins

The great majority of euphorbiaceae we grow in our gardens are tough characters undaunted by frost. Most take cover underground only to re-appear early in the New Year, though a few are evergreen. Some of the large shrub-like evergreen spurges, such as *E. mellifera* (the honey spurge from the Canary Islands) and *E. characias* (from the Mediterranean), can be disfigured by severe cold. On the other hand, their lowly cousin *E. myrsinites*, a ground-hugging spurge from south-eastern Europe and Asia Minor, comes through unscathed. It is one of the

first to flower, bearing heads of yellow bracts, sometimes tinged with orange, at the end of long, scrambling stems clothed in spiralling glaucous leaves. On a dry, sun-baked site, *E. myrsinites* can be backed by tough characters, evolved similarly to enjoy sunbathing and to tolerate drought. Try *Primula auricula* 'Old Mustard' and *Stipa tenuissima* (a wafty fluffy grass), contrasted brilliantly with the spiky bracts of blue forms of *Eryngium bourgatii* and maybe a succulent purple-leafed sedum or two.

Herbaceous species are precocious, providing encouraging glimpses of spring. Some of the earliest are species from The Himalayas – *E. griffithii* and *E. sikkimensis* begin to rocket up amongst the snowdrops. Low at first, by the time they begin to flower from the end of May their stems can reach a metre high. Both have spreading roots whereas *E. palustris* makes big, bold clumps and, though it increases in stature each year, it does not wander. Here at Glebe Cottage we grow masses of *E. palustris*, much of it in our hotbeds. Although it hardly qualifies as hot, its lime-green coloration is a perfect foil for the vivid reds and oranges, which paint these borders. Come the autumn, though, *E. palustris* changes its character and colours – it becomes a burning bush with its willowy stems alight. I'm never sure whether to cut back this spurge after its initial fireworks – it can become ungainly, but as it makes such a brilliant show later it is usually left to its own devices.

Two of the most versatile spurges, coping with sun or shade and thriving in a variety of soils, are *E. polychroma*, a deciduous species

OPPOSITE TOP
Staking *Euphorbia palustris* to ensure it makes maximum impact.

OPPOSITE BELOW
Frost brings an extra dimension to the sprawling stems of *Euphorbia myrsinites*, emphasising their geometry.

with vivid-yellow bracts, and *E.* × *martinii*. *E. polychroma* is an outstanding spurge which can be put to a hundred uses in the April garden. One cultivar, *E. polychroma* 'Major', even flowers again in the summer. It's beautiful with orange tulips, such as 'Princess Irene', and a backdrop of purple elder. *E.* × *martinii* is a handsome hybrid between our native wood spurge and the Mediterranean *E. characias*, an evergreen with red stems and eyes. Because of its parentage, it is suitable for both sunny and shady sites. It is a spurge with great personality, standing about 60cm (2ft) high with dark-crimson foliage and heads of brilliant lime-green flowers with red eyes. Try it with *Milium effusum* 'Aureum', Bowles's golden grass, a few plants of *Primula* Gold-laced Group, whose dark-crimson petal colour picks up on the eyes of the spurge, and *Rheum* 'Ace of Hearts' with crimson reverses to its leaves. The subspecies *Euphorbia amygdaloides* var. *robbiae* has a different habit, running around freely, and is an excellent ground-cover plant for a difficult site – one for any garden.

When you want clones of the self-same plant, cuttings are your only option since it's well nigh impossible to divide euphorbias. Don Witton, one of the euphorbia national collection holders, showed us his method – take side shoots (or sever the central/apical shoot), gently remove the basal leaves, then dib the cutting into a general-purpose compost. Don puts a plastic bag over his cuttings and wears rubber gloves to protect his skin from the irritant sap.

Both species and many cultivars can be grown from seed and, though seedlings may vary, it is a worthwhile way of making more plants. Seedpods are hard, spherical capsules and when ripe explode, flinging the seed often many yards from the mother plant. Several times I've tried to collect seed from euphorbias to no avail. Until it is absolutely ready, the seedpod is impenetrable – even a club hammer doesn't help. The best way to collect seed is to wait for the first seeds to start pinging, then, on a hot day (seed usually ripens in July), place a paper bag over the entire head of seedpods. Tie securely at its base, wait for numerous explosions (you can actually hear the seed pinging) and then separate seed from the residue of the seedcoat and sow it straightaway. Seeds are big enough to be station sown, one to a module compartment, and this is the best way to sow them since they seem to dislike root disturbance. Germination is usually fairly rapid.

OPPOSITE TOP LEFT
Ricinus grows apace, soon becoming an exciting spectacle.
TOP RIGHT
Small plants are pricked out individually and given full light.
BELOW LEFT
The magic beans of *Ricinus communis*, hand-painted. Keep away from children – they're deadly.
BELOW RIGHT
In context, helping create a tropical effect in our hot borders.

Onions

Sometimes you can smell wild garlic, ramsons, before you see it. But when it hoves into view it comes in sheets, in waves surging down slopes and asserting itself in a great tide. Its simple, deep-green leaves make a handsome carpet, and when its starry white flowers open above them it is even more arresting. Its botanical name is *Allium ursinum*, also known, amongst a litany of common names, as bear's onions and badger's plant. Badgers are closely related to bears, and it's easy to imagine both creatures rambling around amongst its vast, viridian swathes. Its country name is used in many place names throughout the British Isles, showing its long association with mankind and the extent of its colonization. It was a bit of a disappointment to find out that one of my favourite Lancashire towns, Ramsbottom, also takes its name from the plant.

In recent times its leaves (in season, naturally) have become an in-vogue ingredient in nouvelle cuisine, and it fits in well with the fashion for foraging that has become an obsession with certain sectors of society. It spreads efficiently by seed and increase of its bulbs – all alliums are essentially bulbs.

Another wild culinary allium is chives, *Allium schoenoprasum*. It's often considered to be a plant introduced by the Romans, but according to Richard Mabey in *Flora Britannica* it is definitely native to the British Isles. As well as being a delicious addition to potato salad, its mild though characteristic flavour has wide uses in the kitchen. Fifty years ago an Alaskan boyfriend rustled up one of the simplest and quickest suppers ever on a camp fire at the foot of the Old Man of Coniston: mashed potato with chopped-up chives and a couple of local eggs, fried. A memorable meal. In the vegetable garden chives are valued as an edging plant, neat and decorative with their pretty pink flowers.

Cultivated cousins

Just as ramsons have become de rigueur in the kitchen, so ornamental alliums have risen to the top of the list of must-have plants in the garden.

They have become hugely popular, featuring frequently in show gardens at the RHS Chelsea and Hampton Court Flower Shows, and widely popularised in the gardening press. One year, the RHS chose an allium as its logo in all the publicity for Chelsea, and surely the best bulb-

ABOVE
Chives, one of our most versatile wild herbs, could be grown just for its floral beauty – drumsticks of purple flowers.

OPPOSITE
Ramsons, wild garlic, *Allium schoenoprasum*. Whatever you call, it you can smell it from yards away.

merchants in the country, Avon Bulbs, have a beautiful sculpture of an allium seedhead in the centre of their displays.

It is alliums' sculptural structure, even more than their colour, that has made them so appreciated. Both in flower and in seed, their usually tall stems support a pom-pom of small flowers. Sometimes it is a lollipop, sometimes a starburst, but almost invariably a sphere. The individual flowers within each head take their place, symmetrically arranged to ensure each flower has an equal opportunity of being pollinated.

My friend Andrew Lawson, the wonderful plant photographer, had a good idea about making the most of allium seedheads. When they were in seed and still standing to attention, he would cut their stems close to the ground, invert them and hang them up to dry indoors. When winter comes the wonderful structures of these ornamental onions tend to become bedraggled and misshapen, but this cunning ruse ensured they were in prime condition. Andrew would take them out and arrange them in his winter garden to great effect. One of the most effective for this use is *A. cristophii*, with

huge spherical heads composed of scores of starry flowers. Any of the alliums will keep their seedheads, but *A. cristophii*, *A. aflatunense* and *A. giganteum* have the most impact.

Most alliums thrive in a sunny site and well-drained soil. Although they have first-class flowers, almost without exception their foliage is second-rate. They need companions which will hide their basal shame, provide a perfect foil to show off their bold globes and assert their primacy as the flowers fade, still providing scaffolding for the seedheads. Interesting foliage can be the key, and the bold leaves of hostas or rodgersias would work with the purple spheres suspended above. *Chaerophyllum hirsutum* 'Roseum', a pink cow-parsley relative, flowers at much the same time as *A. hollandicum* – because the pink of its umbels of tiny flowers has blue in it there is real empathy between them. What's more, the rich-green ferny leaves of the chaerophyllum hide a multitude of sins both before and after the allium's climax.

Not all alliums are big and bold, and if you garden in pots, or have limited space, there are a host of smaller, neater plants, wonderful popping up between alpines or grown as individuals in their own special container. We have grown *A. beesianum* here at Glebe Cottage for years and, though it manages to fend for itself and increase gradually, when it is grown in its own terracotta pot you can really appreciate its considerable charms. Its leaves are grassy, bright green and needle thin, and make the perfect foil for the copious heads of dainty bright-blue flowers. A real fairy plant.

OPPOSITE TOP LEFT
Some onions are just plain funny. This walking onion makes everyone smile.
TOP RIGHT
The silken starburst of *Allium cristophii* is a

masterpiece of geometric construction.
OPPOSITE BELOW
Allium sphaerocephalon dancing through the prickly blue stars of *Eryngium* × *zabelii*. Some plants are just meant to party.

A. flavum is one of those plants which, once you've seen it, you just have to grow. Dainty, glaucous stems about 20cm (8in) high support heads of lemon-yellow flowers that open at different times to create a Roman-candle sort of effect. It creates splashes of scintillating, citric colour in July when most rock gardens seem to have fallen asleep, waking them up from the late-summer doldrums.

At the top of our shady garden there is a platform that juts out into the sunshine. There is no real soil here, but the space is covered with pea gravel and has no doubt collected residual debris from the trees round about. In it have seeded a host of *A. pulchellum* (its name means beautiful, and it is). The majority are purple, but here and there the exquisite white form, *A. pulchellum f. album,* has made bright highlights. Thriving on neglect this happy, self-sustaining community is one of the prettiest sights in the July garden.

Though there are some alliums that can be divided, chives and wild garlic being two of the most obvious examples, most of us introduce them into our gardens as dry bulbs. Sometimes they are big bulbs, often quite expensive as in *A. giganteum,* sometimes though they are relatively cheap. You can make a real show of *A. sphaerocephalon* (the round-headed leek, although its flowerheads are more egg-shaped than spherical) for a few pounds. Weave it amongst clump-forming perennials, including geraniums and their ilk. Those with more willowy stems, *Gaura lindheimeri* or amsonia, are equally effective partners, too. Planting about

8cm (3in) deep in odd numbers and in random positions works best.

Almost all alliums fare best in a sunny situation and fertile soil, appreciating good drainage. Atypically wild garlic thrives best in damp woodland. The majority of these ornamental onions are hardy but growing them in pots in a wet, cold winter can lead to devastation. We once grew *A. christophii* one to a pot, hoping to use their delightful starburst flowers in our Chelsea Flower Show display. Out of 100 we got five, the other 95 turned to soggy, onion-scented mush. It was an exceptionally cold, wet winter and the pots were standing on a concrete base with no efficient drainage. We have never lost them in the ground where they have the protection of soil both around and above their bulbs, and where excess moisture can drain away. If your soil is on the heavy side it's worth digging in extra grit before planting and incorporating even more at the base of each planting hole.

Ferns

Wandering through the woods at the end of April or early in May fills you with an excitement that is almost primeval. The cerebral is forgotten, you don't think it, you feel it – you immerse yourself in a landscape that must have changed little for thousands of years. And the plants that contribute most to this sense of immediacy, of the visceral as opposed to the mental or intellectual, have been around much longer – not thousands, but millions of years. During that time they have changed little, having carved out for themselves a niche and evolved a survival strategy that is indestructible. There is a smell attached to them, an indescribable odour of earth and all that is fundamental about the soil and what grows in it. At once it is the smell of decay and that of life. Creatures, and eventually men, encountering the smell must always have recognised it. It is not only the smell of ferns that is singular but their sexuality too. They do not set seed in the way that most other plants do, yet they reproduce successfully in many cases prodigiously.

Ferns are amongst the oldest plants on the Earth. Their ancestry stretches back five hundred million years, and makes flowering plants look like newcomers who have just tipped up. Although fern species may have evolved continuously during this time (there are as many as 10,000 species, only 50 of which occur in the British Isles), their sex-life has remained unchanged. And a very esoteric sex-life it is. Flowering plants reproduce each generation from seed, but ferns have no flowers and set no seed. It is because of this practice, unexplained until the invention of microscopes, that ferns have had a mystical, almost magical significance. Because they have evolved a strategy for reproduction without flowers and seed they are seeped in mythology. Shakespeare even mentions them in *King Henry IV* (Act 2, Scene 1): 'We have the receipt of fern seed, we walk invisible.' On Midsummer's Eve, at midnight, spores were collected in pewter dishes to bestow the gift of invisibility. Ferns have long associations with witchcraft and magic. The fact that they are plants that need no direct light adds to the intrigue.

In one corner of our garden, underneath a line of tall beeches planted as a farm hedge long ago, there is little light and yet the place

ABOVE
Like fists, the furled fronds of ferns are packed with latent energy.

OPPOSITE
When they explode, nothing can stop them.

breathes life and verdancy. There are the beech leaves themselves that tell the story of the year. From unscrolling buds dispersing the pink fluff of their leaf casings over the soil, to the leaves themselves – transparent, lime-green at first, deep-viridian in late summer and later glorious gold and amber. Later the dark soil and green moss are emblazoned with the orange and mahogany of the beeches' fallen leaves and their fruit. Underneath the beeches, once they have spread their canopy, there is little chance of growing flowers; they would be out of place anyway. These same sort of conditions must exist in so many gardens, not necessarily in the shade of giant beeches but often that of houses, garages, sheds, or the overhanging branches of 'weed trees' or leylandii hedges.

Ferns of all descriptions thrive in such dark corners, but from November onwards the evergreen varieties come into their own. They persist through the winter and, provided they have some shelter from the coldest winds, their fronds will look as pristine on New Year's Day as they did in midsummer. Many of them are native to the British Isles, some are from Europe and Asia, South America and even Australasia. They combine perfectly, and the variety of their individual fronds, from solid and shiny to soft and lacy, adds a wealth of textural interest.

OPPOSITE
Throughout the garden at Glebe Cottage ferns make themselves at home, always finding a spot where they look meant to be.

Cultivated cousins

Devon, where we live, is famous for its ferns. During the Victorian era, fern trains would leave regularly from the North Devon coast for London, their wagons packed with ferns stripped from the north-facing slopes and hedgerows to satisfy the fern craze that swept the capital. Thankfully ferns are survivors and there is little evidence now of these former depredations. The high Devon banks positively drip with *Polypodium vulgare*, one of the most enduring and most useful of evergreen ferns. It spreads slowly outwards establishing large colonies. On a bank its stoloniferous roots bind the soil together and create pockets where mosses and primroses can make a home. The individual fronds, about 30cm (12in) long, are deeply cut and a bright, fresh green. Even when this fern is butchered by mechanical hedge trimmers, its fronds quickly re-sprout, repairing the bruised and battered hedgerow. One variety, *P. interjectum* 'Cornubiense' has finely cut fronds. Sometimes it reverts, and the typical, plainer fronds re-assert themselves – when this happens they should be removed promptly.

Polypodium is often accompanied by the upright shuttlecocks of *Asplenium scolopendrium*, the hart's tongue fern. Although it is not much taller than the polypodium, asplenium creates a much more architectural effect. It contrasts well with low, clumping plants and the lacy filigree of many other ferns. It appears frequently at Glebe Cottage, usually at the base of walls making a living 'skirting board'. There are several variations on the theme including

A. scolopendrium Crispum Cristatum Group, a highly prized variety whose undulating edges give it a frilly look.

If you need a bold fern with glossy, dark-green fronds that stands up for itself and achieves a metre in height, then *Blechnum chilense* should be ideal. It comes from Chile, and under normal conditions in a British garden it will gradually colonise. Under trees or in a sheltered corner it has protection from the worst of the weather, but it might turn its toes up in a really cold garden. It has been frozen solid here from time to time, but it has always managed to get going again. *Blechnum spicant* is a native plant, half the size of its Chilean cousin but just as beautiful. Sometimes it is adorned with taller, slimmer fronds which bear the spores.

The famous lady gardener, Gertrude Jekyll, wrote that 'green is also a colour', and the greens of ferns cover so wide a range of greens, no two ever seeming the same. But there are a few evergreen ferns whose fronds are definitely not green. When *Dryopteris erythrosora* unfurls its new fronds they are decidedly orange – it almost looks autumnal although this new growth pushes through during April and May. Its fronds are glossy and eventually the orange changes to rich green. They are beautifully arched, and just one plant set against a tree stump makes a fine picture. This is an exceptionally beautiful fern, and it comes as no surprise that it originates in China and Japan. *Dryopteris dilatata*, our native broad buckler fern, is just as graceful but deciduous.

The shield ferns, polystichum, contribute several very varied species to the evergreen ferns available to grace our shady corners. *Polystichum setiferum*, the soft shield fern, is one of my all-time favourites, especially *P. setiferum* Acutilobum Group and *P. setiferum* 'Divisilobum Densum'. Both are elegant and very finely cut, creating a frothy effect. The central midrib of each frond is covered with shaggy brown scales, and the fronds themselves are of a lovely soft green.

No matter whether you have room for just one of these beautiful ferns, or a stumpery with numerous examples of each species, once they take up residence in your garden they give an air of timelessness, an echo of the primeval.

Polystichum setiferum occasionally produces bulbils along its central stem. The variety *P. setiferum* 'Proliferum Wollaston' reliably produces them, and if they are separated and potted they soon form plantlets. Alternatively a whole frond can be detached and pinned down on a tray of good compost, or in the garden still attached to the plant. When the plantlets have their own roots, they can be potted up individually. Growing ferns from spores is explained in my book *Grow Your Own Garden* – it is a painstaking business but well worth it.

OPPOSITE
These shuttlecock ferns are in the shade all day, but when the setting sun lights up their fronds, they're transformed.

Fritillaries

The first time I saw *Fritillaria meleagris* is ingrained in my memory. It was forty years ago, at Kew Gardens on a clear-skyed April day. Neil and I had bicycled from our home in Ladbroke Grove – quite a long ride – and I was determined to lap up everything I could find. One solitary snake's head fritillary had seeded itself in an unlikely place; it was bewitching, a perfect bell with seemingly hand-painted tessellations – was this a practical joke? Touching the waxy petals of the flower confirmed its authenticity, and when the bell was turned upwards it was even more astonishing – the pattern continued and the petals were further decorated by glistening nectaries attached to them.

Meleagris means spotted, like a guinea fowl, and all the vernacular names given to the flower, from death bell to leopard's lily, allude to its sinister colouring and bizarre patterning. It is the only species of fritillary indigenous to the British Isles, but even then some think it was originally a garden escapee. It is a meadow

plant, and would once have been a common constituent of the luscious mixture of perennial flowers, bulbs and sweet grasses that made up an average water meadow.

During the winter and early spring, low-lying land alongside rivers would have been deliberately flooded to enrich the soil, often dammed with the branches of the crack willow that frequently grows along the banks of rivers and streams. The residue of minerals and nutrients left behind when the water subsided would feed ragged robin, lady's smock, meadow buttercups and fritillaries. By the time the meadows were cut for hay, seed would have been set and distributed far and wide by summer breezes. Although the snake's head fritillary flowers at only a foot or so, the stems lengthen to as much as 60cm (2ft) as the seed capsules swell. This enables the neatly stacked, wafer-thin seed, its seedpod upright by now, to cast itself around as its papery sheath splits into sections. *Fritillaria meleagris* is happy in any garden setting providing it has ample moisture and humus-rich soil, but looks best planted informally.

Cultivated cousins
All fritillaries are fascinating. From the tall, majestic stems of *Fritillaria imperialis* to the

ABOVE
The snake's head fritillary as it must once have grown in damp meadows – by the thousands.

OPPOSITE
Individually, every flower of *Fritillaria meleagris* is intriguing yet sinister.

bewitching tessellated bells of the snake's head fritillary, each species is as beguiling as the next. There are rare and special fritillaries; species such as the red-flowered *Fritillaria pudica*, brought to perfection over many years to take its place on the show bench to the admiring 'oohs' and 'ahs' of a fascinated audience. Such plants need very particular treatment, and are the province of experts. For we ordinary mortals there are a host of species and cultivars that will thrive under normal garden conditions with the minimum of cosseting. As with any other group of plants, the key to success is to select those best suited to the soil and situation.

Far and away the most spectacular, the crown imperial (*Fritillaria imperialis*) often graces the front gardens of small cottages where it may have grown for scores of years. There is something quirkily incongruous about the presence of this great majestic flower in such modest surroundings – we are more used to seeing it in the context of grandiose Dutch flower paintings of the seventeenth century. Its whorls of large bells in rusty oranges and vivid reds and yellows encircle stout yard-high stems finished off with a tuffet of leaves reminiscent of a pineapple.

Others are much more subtle beauties. They impress by understatement. Many have refined bells in bronze, yellow or green. Often the colours are combined within one flower, and the bells are frequently marked with fine lines and tessellations to create further nuances of pattern and subtle texture. One of the easiest and most readily available is *Fritillaria uva-vulpis*, from Iraq, Iran and Turkey where it is a cornfield and meadow plant. Although it might survive amongst low grass it will do better in an open sunny site in well-drained soil. Its flowers are chocolate-brown edged in golden yellow.

Fritillaria acmopetala is also common in cornfields in the Middle East. Its comparatively large bells of pale jade-green are marked with maroon blotches, each hanging from a dainty shepherd's-crook stem and with the base of the petals curiously pointed and slightly flexed. It is one of the most elegant species and a fabulous garden plant.

From the meadows of the Pyrenees, *Fritillaria pyrenaica* announces itself in an even quieter voice. It is very variable (one of the charms of all these small fritillaries) although as a generality its bells are brown, with subtle tessellations in richer brown, and each one is edged in golden yellow. It will seed itself around if seedheads are allowed to ripen and cast their contents about. There is a yellow form, which is quite a rarity, but this does not necessarily seed true. All these species will be happy in good, fertile but

OPPOSITE TOP LEFT
Black and beautiful, the big bells of *Fritillaria camschatcensis*.
TOP RIGHT
F. michailovskyi. Surely hats for fairies, edged in gold.

BELOW LEFT
The muted flowers of *Fritillaria verticillata*. Quiet and unassuming on the outside but inside what riches!
BELOW RIGHT
F. p. 'Adiyaman'. When it flowers well it has a unique magic.

well-drained soil, in sunny niches where they are not in direct competition from robust and overpowering perennials.

Fritillaria pontica is another easy self-seeder, but is also likely to proliferate by a different method. Many fritillaries produce 'rice' – tiny bulbils spontaneously produced and clustered around the bulb. In time this rice will grow and swell until the bulbs reach flowering size. This can happen without any intervention, but if the infant bulbs are lifted, potted (in a loam-based soil with plenty of extra grit) and allowed to grow on outside, they will reach maturity faster.

Similar conditions suit Fritillaria camschatcensis. This is one of the most alluring of all fritillaries. Its slate-blue flowers atop foot-high stems have a grape-like bloom. Fritillaria persica 'Adiyaman' shares the same dusty damson colouring but is even more striking. Its numerous bells are arranged around stems up to 75cm (2½ft) tall and make a devastatingly gorgeous combination with the whorls of glaucous foliage. It can be a frustrating plant (even when carefully planted some stems appear devoid of flowers), but when it performs well there is nothing to touch it – its bulbs are huge. Wol and Sue Staines, of Glen Chantry, describe buying bulbs at an Alpine Garden Society sale wrapped in tin foil 'like baked potatoes'. Presumably the idea was to keep the bulbs fat and firm to prevent them from becoming dry and desiccated.

For reliable performance give fritillaries what they like. Work grit or lime rubble into soil for those that appreciate sharp drainage,

including Fritillaria uva-vulpis, F. acmopetala, F. pyrenaica, F. michailovskyi and the delightful North American F. biflora 'Martha Roderick'.

In common with other members of the lily family, fritillary bulbs are composed of a series of overlapping scales and frequently the centre of the bulb is hollow. When planting the large bulbs (they can be as big as a grapefruit) of F. persica 'Adiyaman' or crown imperials, especially in the rich moist earth that they prefer, it is good practice to plant them on their side. This cuts down the chances of water settling in the centre of the bulb, causing it to rot. Both shoots and roots will make their own way despite the disorientation. F. pallidiflora and F. camschatcensis also appreciate deep, fertile soil which does not dry out and will take some shade.

Always plant deeply, with the depth of soil above the bulb twice that of the size of the bulb. If you are planting dormant bulbs, make sure they are firm. Sometimes you can buy fritillaries in growth, which is an excellent way to ensure you have the right thing and to work out what company to give them.

Larger fritillaries can be propagated just like lilies, by removing their scales and inducing small bulbs to grow at their base (see my book Grow Your Own Garden, p136). You can collect the seed of smaller species and sow it thinly in trays.

OPPOSITE
The crown imperial, so aptly named – stately and majestic.

EARLY SUMMER

There's no dividing line between spring and summer but, one day, you go out of the house, feel the warm sun on the back of your neck, sniff the soft air and know it's here. There may be frosts, unexpected and sometimes cruel, but you know that this is just the winter loathe to give up, the holly king exerting the dregs of his waning power as the oak king steps into the picture and takes command.

The flowers of early spring are fresh and jewel-like. Green is the overriding colour, but now it gives way to a kaleidoscope of flower. If spring is the new beginning then early summer is the start of the party. The bunting is up, there's music to dance to. Let the celebrations begin.

Every hedgerow, motorway embankment and city park bursts into a froth of blossom, underlaid by curtains of translucent green as hawthorn, cherry, apple and beech rev up. Our gardens explode into growth.

Summer is it. The culmination of all the planning and planting, no more to be done for the moment than enjoy. The earth is warm. Watered by copious amounts of spring rain and encouraged by longer days of clear light, plants grow apace.

Day after day there are fresh suprises, new enjoyments. Some are individuals, pushing themselves forward insistently. Oriental poppies shout loudest. Their big, blowsy blooms cannot be ignored. Each flouncy flower lasts only a day or two but what it lacks in longevity it makes up for in concentrated *va-va-voom*. The garden is full of frothy umbels, of astrantias and Jacob's ladder, tumbling beside all the easy-going plants that make this the most carefree time of the year.

Our meadow cranesbill weaves its blue magic amongst the burgeoning grasses, crested dog's-tail and Yorkshire fog, while dog roses and the first of the honeysuckles scramble along hedgerows festooned in blossom and new leaves. Dog daisies lift their heads on high, singing in the sun, accompanied here and there by swathes of blood red poppies. The bells of foxgloves vibrate with the sound of fat bumble bees making their escape. On sunny days the air is abuzz with insects, everything is busy, positive. The first butterflies are on the wing, peacocks flutter from flower to flower and along the lane and in the newly emerged canopy of the beech trees, speckled woods chase each other. Love is in the air. Along road verges the tide of cow-parsley swells and spumes, reaching symphonic proportions.

Summer is a coming in.

Hawthorn

May is effervescent, the most ebullient month of all. It's a time for celebration, for dancing, full of the songs of birds, the froth and freshness of blossom and green growth and the exultation of spring's achievement as it bows out, passing on its legacy to the advent of fast-approaching summer.

All around the skirts of every field are avalanches of hawthorn blossom, intensifying the feeling of newness that abounds throughout nature. The sensation of newness is so overriding it makes your heart beat faster. Here are leaves that have never ever been seen before, in awe I soak up their greenness, their transparency. The garden is full of miracles.

Along Pixie Lane at the top of the track, hawthorn leaves have been blown off the trees and drift in bright green flotillas across the puddles, the east wind whipping up ripples and driving them to the edges where they lie beached. They are such tender young leaves (purportedly good on sandwiches too). Where

I come from we call hawthorn 'May' after the month when it flowers, and though there must be weeks of difference countrywide between the first and the last buds opening, it is beloved by all. It emblazons hedges and verges in the countryside and along motorways, and its froth of effervescent blossom softens many a post-industrial landscape obliterating, or at least mellowing, the scars of coal tips and slag heaps.

Perhaps because hawthorn is so ubiquitous, we tend to undervalue it – familiarity breeds contempt, yet this is one of the most valuable small trees any of us could nurture in our gardens. It is characterful, each one has its own personality, and, if you choose to plant the native tree *Crataegus monogyna*, you will introduce an individual to your garden that may well outlive you, your children and your children's children. Hawthorns are amongst the most long-lived trees there are and one of the most useful to wildlife. Their abundant blossom provides nectar and pollen for numerous insects. It has two scents – one is a sweet perfume, evolved perhaps to attract bees and hoverflies. The other is not so much a scent as a smell, and presumably broadens the range of potential pollinators to include dung flies and the like! Once these insects have got

ABOVE
Hawthorn higs – these berries will adorn the prickly branches right through into the winter.

OPPOSITE
'May' blossom is the frothiest of all.

to work and the flowers are pollinated, the red berries or haws that the tree sets are one of autumn's treats. Again we humans are not the most important beneficiaries! Blackbirds and thrushes feast on them and there are still plenty left when flocks of redwings and fieldfares fly in from their northern summer haunts to enjoy a warmer winter here.

Haws, or higs as we call them in Lancashire, last for ages. They are hard, single-seeded fruit, ideal ammunition for catapults as my brothers proved in our younger days. Often hawthorns were planted close to oaks. There is a beautiful example of this association in the field we look across to from the cottage – the oak cradles the hawthorn. Long may they flourish.

If you have room for only one tree a native hawthorn is an attractive proposition, though seldom considered or recommended by gardening pundits. It will need no special attention and within just a few years will have started to display its own individuality. Traditionally lone thorns are known as 'fairy trees' – the place where fairies gather, or sometimes in which they live, and as such it is considered unlucky to cut them down or damage them. Of all native trees it is the hawthorn, both in France and in the British

Isles, that is most deeply steeped in folklore and most of the stories and superstitions attached to it are to do with when it flowers. It signifies the essence of the passing of spring into summer and was used extensively in May Day ceremonies. The Puritans hated it – no doubt the pagans loved it.

We have hawthorn in the hedges that surround the garden and we included lots of it when we planted our native hedge many years ago. I planted a cultivar, *Crataegus laevigata* 'Paul's Scarlet', in the garden proper and wish that I hadn't. Though it is a bonny tree its pretty double-pink blossom offers nothing to insects – they are not a patch on the fresh and fluffy flowers of true May.

Cultivated cousins

Hawthorn is one of the constituents of many hedges and if you haven't room for a full-grown tree, a native hedge is an option even in small gardens.

Traditionally British gardens have clear and distinct boundaries. Not only are they designed to delineate the exact extent of the space, but they act as barriers, almost fortifications, to keep others out. Many are walls or fences and where there are hedges they are liable to be almost as lifeless as any man-made construction – witness the pandemic of leylandii hedges famously visible from outer space or the privet that outlines our city streets. More of us may be extending a welcome to wildlife by creating ponds and planting wild flowers, but our hospitality often comes to an abrupt halt at

OPPOSITE
The best of friends. This towering oak hugs the hawthorn, seeming to offer it protection.

the boundaries of our gardens. A native hedge, however, offers a wealth of food for creatures at every level of the food chain, and provides shelter for insects, birds and small mammals.

Native trees and shrubs are perfectly at home in our gardens. They want to grow, and making them into a hedge gives you the opportunity to include a range of species in a limited space – the more you include the more varied the visitors and residents. Taking account of your soil and the situation improves success – spindle, *Euonymus europaeus*, for example, prefers alkaline soil, whereas rowan, *Sorbus aucuparia*, flourishes in acid soils.

Crataegus monogyna is one of the most vital plants to include. An important food plant, its flowers, leaves and berries are essential fare for many insects, their larvae and for birds and small mammals. It is often known as quickthorn because of its rapidity, and this coupled with dense, thorny growth, frothy flowers (rich in nectar) and bird-magnet berries make it numero uno. Marry it with beech, *Fagus sylvatica*, which is at its most evocative in late spring with translucent, fresh-green leaves. Old leaves persist on hedge beech, adding rich winter colour and important asylum.

Hazel, *Corylus avellana*, has been used as a hedge and coppice tree for aeons. Its lamb's-tail catkins delight children and, once established, it can be raided for twiggy pea sticks.

Field maple, *Acer campestre*, provides splashes of vivid autumn colour, while *Viburnum opulus* has outstanding flowers and luscious berries. Common holly, *Ilex aquifolium*, is the best

evergreen to include. Male and female plants are needed for good berrying. Oak, *Quercus robur*, hosts more creatures than any other tree. Plant some acorns.

Young bare-root trees (one or two years old) may look insubstantial to start with but will rapidly overtake older, more expensive, pot-grown specimens. Sprinkling mycorrhizal fungi amongst the roots encourages them to take in nutrients and establish faster. Prepare the ground well and remove any perennial weeds. Plant 45cm (18in) apart, water well and weed frequently.

You can grow wild flowers and grasses at its feet and it will provide the perfect support for native climbers. Dog roses, honeysuckle, bryony and ivy will clamber through it, embellishing the tapestry and making it richer still. The more species you include, the wider the diversity of creatures it will attract.

Planting a native hedge can turn a boundary into an ever-changing source of life and beauty, and rather than creating a barrier it can present an open door for wildlife.

OPPOSITE
Our native hedge gets better every year – and all of its own volition.

Bluebells

There are few opportunities nowadays to see wild flowers in unbounded exuberance. They have been marginalized, destroyed and emasculated by 'progress'. But one flower at least still manages to give us some idea of how things were, and just how awe-inspiring wild flowers can be when they hold sway.

Bluebells en masse are an experience, something that is done to you. Rather than a sight from which you can separate yourself, they involve you, wash over you. Every sense is carried away in the flood. Water and bluebells are often associated – we talk about 'a sea of bluebells' or the woodland floor being 'awash with bluebells'. As you'd expect, the sight of bluebells has inspired poets through centuries – Shakespeare, John Clare, Keats, Tennyson and, perhaps best of all, Gerard Manley Hopkins: 'in falls of sky-colour washing the brows and slacks of the ground with vein-blue.'

Though bluebells have been picked by the armful since time immemorial, more damage is done by trampling on their leaves (making it impossible for the bulbs to feed through them) than is done by picking.

Perusing an individual stem from a bluebell is a revelation. The long bells with parallel sides are turned back at the mouth of the bell giving it a fairy's hat appearance – in Somerset it's called blue bonnets. The pollen the bells protect is creamy white, and they dangle gracefully from arching stems all to one side or, as Gerard Manley Hopkins would say, 'all having their heads one way'. Leaves are strong, bright green and succulent, and both they and the stems stick together when they're picked. The bulbs are white, often buried deep in the woodsy soil, and have the capacity to send out new stems underground and form new bulbs. They spread freely from seed too, and can be grown from it (though such seed should be collected from plants far away from Spanish bluebells).

I worry about the wild bluebells in the garden here. Almost all the bluebells in the property next door are Spanish, or hybrids, and since bees are no respecters of boundaries there is every chance that our wild bluebells may become contaminated. The only solution is to keep out an eagle eye for new plants that are obviously hybrids and weed them out, bulbs and all.

We all acknowledge the magic of a bluebell wood but even in a small garden, where acres of bluebells are unachievable, pools of blue can be created which can adorn shady places from midwinter to late spring. Blue is one of the most elusive colours in the garden. For a start it is in short supply – there just aren't masses of blue flowers from which to choose. Apart from their rarity value, there is something extra-special about blue flowers, everyone loves them. Perhaps it has to do with the sky or the sea, something to do with infinity and timelessness. Blue flowers are never in your face, never overpowering, rather they create a feeling of space, of distance. That bright ethereal azure is one of spring's most telling colours, and

OPPOSITE
No blue in the world can surpass that of a bluebell wood in full spate.

the great majority of it is painted by blue bulbs, many of them closely related to bluebells.

Although they themselves won't arrive until later, the image that immediately springs to mind when these bulbs are employed, even in a tiny garden, is one of beech or oak woods carpeted in bluebells. There is nothing obvious about drifts of scilla or chionodoxa, but patches of their luminous blue flowers sprinkled amongst trees and shrubs are an uplifting sight.

Cultivated cousins

At Glebe Cottage we have grown blue bulbs almost from the word go. The rector who used to be our neighbour gave us a few *Chionodoxa luciliae* soon after we came. They had self-seeded all over the garden next door and I was entranced by them. Even the common-a-garden grape hyacinth, *Muscari latifolium*, put itself between the stone steps made when we first arrived, and though it did rather too well it was always a source of delight when you opened the front door.

Chionodoxa sardensis is sometimes referred to as Glory of the Snow. It is early into flower, and I have seen it in Devon pushing its bright blue stars up through snow colonising a little cultivated wood. Each year it increased

(it spreads by seed and offsets) until there was a blue carpet underneath the trees. Plant the bulbs deep but close together. Its brilliant-blue flowers have a small white centre.

Muscari armeniacum, the grape hyacinth, is well known to most gardeners due to its colonising habits. Although it can become invasive it is one of the most amenable of all bulbs, seeding itself graciously in corners where nothing else will grow. Its foliage can be untidy, but the wealth of blue flowers it produces with zero fuss make it a favourite – and it's happy in sun or shade.

Easy and straightforward, *Muscari azureum*, or *M. pseudomuscari*, has charming conical heads of palest-blue flowers that set it apart from the deeper blue of most muscari. Grow it with the silver emerging leaves of *Stachys byzantina*, anaphalis or some of the artemisias. It does best in light soils in an open site, or in containers, sinks or troughs. It looks lovely planted thickly in a line of old clay pots. It is one of the first of these blue bulbs to flower, and oblivious of harsh conditions it can hardly wait to get through the ground and start flowering. It follows the snowdrops, lighting up the garden with its flowers of delicate blue. Plant it in drifts under trees or on a rock garden. It grows slightly taller in shade, and the flowers are less likely to be marred by splashed soil or nibbled by slugs – it naturalises well.

Valerie Finnis was a hugely knowledgeable and inspiring gardener, plantswoman and photographer. She was also a first-rate human being – witty, naughty and fun to be with.

OPPOSITE TOP LEFT
Odd but interesting, *Muscari latifolium* always seems to be in two minds.
TOP RIGHT
'Glory of the Snow' *Chionodoxa* seeds itself around, sprinkling its blue stars hither and thither.
OPPOSITE BELOW
In a shady corner of our garden, true bluebells are encouraged to colonise amongst other spring stars.

Muscari 'Valerie Finnis' has tubular racemes of charming palest-blue flowers that distinguish it from the deeper blue of most muscari. *Muscari* 'Jenny Robinson', often called baby's breath, is similar but has neater leaves – it is fitting somehow that 'Valerie Finnis' is more unruly, not quite so well behaved!

Bulbs that appear early are particularly valuable and *Puschkinia scilloides* var. *libanotica* arrives as the snowdrops fade. Its bright, delicate blue stars, on short stems rising from short broad leaves, are always a reassurance that spring is making progress. Each petal has a charming deeper-blue central stripe. In common with so many members of hyacinthaceae it appears in a rush – invisible one moment and in its full glory the next.

Perfect for a big rock garden or spaces between trees, *Scilla siberica* (the squill) is one of the bluest of all blue flowers. Its individual flowers are bigger than most of the blue bulbs, and although its stems are only a few inches high its luminous colour makes it very visible. It is usually offered as *Scilla* 'Spring Beauty'. The bulbs are relatively large and each one produces several flowering stems.

It's always good to have a few amusing plants in the garden, and *Muscari* 'Plumosum' is just that. Each of its stacks of blue flowers is finished off with a tuft or tassle of bright-purple plumes. These strange flowers are sterile and evolved to lure pollinating insects. There are other even more bizarre forms including *Muscari armeniacum* 'Fantasy Creation' with flowers like purple-sprouting broccoli. Enough said.

There need to be plenty of them to make a real splash. Most are cheap enough and, as well as dividing themselves and increasing slowly underground, many seed themselves about. Unlike bigger bulbs, such as lillies where seedlings may take many years to build themselves up into large bulbs, these small blue bulbs can reach flowering size in a couple of years.

Many of the species are woodlanders perfectly at home amongst tree roots, but most are versatile and can cope with sunnier spots. Tough and robust, some species originate from the Mediterranean region and Turkey where they often grow high in the mountains. Most are perfect for pot cultivation but none need warmth or shelter to open up their bonny blue blooms.

To create a natural effect they can be scattered here and there or handfuls can be thrown up in the air and planted exactly where they land. When planting amongst tree roots, it pays to be circumspect and to investigate first with a small hand fork before plunging a trowel into the ground. All that is needed when planting is a handful or two of leaf mould mixed with the excavated soil. The planting hole should be three times as deep as the bulb and even in heavy soils there is no need to incorporate grit.

OPPOSITE TOP
Planting *Muscari armeniacum* 'Valerie Finnis' in our 'sea-side garden'. The soil here is impoverished and well-drained.
BELOW
In years to come it will spread itself around.

Buttercups

When we came here 34 years ago there had never been a garden. Perennial weeds were in complete control and one of the most tenacious was the creeping buttercup, *Ranunculus repens*. Nonetheless when it opened its golden, glossy goblets they were as appealing as any cultivated flower – simple, direct and joyous.

Buttercups of every description revel in the wet, heavy clay here, plunging their roots deep into the cleggy, fertile soil. In the fields and road verges roundabout, the true meadow buttercup, *Ranunculus acris*, casts a brilliant yellow aura amongst and above the meadow grasses with whom it is so much at home. There are still fields that for a month or more of the early summer are transformed into great gilded spaces by its glossy open chalices. Despite the vividness of its flowers they always fit in, unlike the lurid and often shocking brilliance of rape. They are always at home, the rich chrome-yellow of their petals tempered by the greenness of the grass, especially rich during late May and June. They

are meadow flowers par excellence, and many of their country names allude to cows, butter and cream.

Not only do you associate herds of dairy cattle chomping through their midst, but you can imagine a time when cutting the verdant grasses, and the wild flowers that grew with them for hay, was part of the cycle of the year.

Both my great-grandfathers on my father's side were, at one time, corn-cutters, which means they would have been hay-cutters too. How different their lives must have been.

Cultivated cousins

Nowadays the creeping buttercup that used to flourish here is banished to the wildest edges of the garden, but other, better-behaved, less overbearing members of its family are welcomed. Many are at home in shade. Wet shade is just as problematic as dry shade, and finding solutions just as exciting.

The buttercup family (ranunculaceae) offers a wealth of very beautiful plants, most of which flower between Easter and midsummer. Many have the glowing golden flowers of my creeping buttercup, others are paler-yellow and occasionally white. Aconites and delphiniums represent the blue side of the spectrum and flower much later than the spring buttercups. Most aconites will thrive in dappled shade in

ABOVE
Buttercups are the archetypal meadow plant, luxuriating in the mixed company of other flowers and grasses.
OPPOSITE
Do you like butter?

heavy soil, whereas delphiniums need more sun. *Aconitum carmichaelii* makes clumps of lustrous bronzed foliage in the early spring. From July onwards flower spikes emerge pushing up to 90cm or 1.2m (3 or 4ft) encased in rich-blue, hooded flowers.

Heavy wet soils are bliss for the plants that have evolved to cope with them. Most have extensive root systems and fleshy, thong-like roots, which can absorb water without rotting. Many can even cope with inundation – trollius and caltha often grow beside rivers that flood and still come out smiling. The fact that they adore the cool afforded by trees such as alders and willows make them doubly useful.

Ranunculus aconitifolius 'Flore Pleno' has been in cultivation for centuries. It has numerous common names, fair maids of France, fair maids of Kent and bachelor's buttons, for instance, indicating that it has been widely grown and beloved by gardeners. When plants have so many names and enjoy such popularity it is usually a mark of their garden-worthiness. No wonder. Its dainty spherical flowers of pristine white evenly decorate branching stems rising to about 45cm (18in). It has a neat, tailored look about it, almost too good to be true, whereas the single species, *Ranunculus aconitifolius*, has a wild

and wayward charm. Both single and double belong to the group of plants I like to think of as Cinderellas – plants that go to sleep during the summer and wake up each spring to furnish our gardens.

The single-flowered *Ranunculus aconitifolius* frequents damp mountain meadows. It relishes heavy wet ground. I have plenty of that and each spring it treats me to a breathtaking show of airy, branching stems twinkling with a galaxy of diminutive white buttercups. It is light-hearted, frivolous even, and has a wildness which is very seductive. Its double-flowered sibling is a much more civilised individual. More showy too, with exquisite white pom-poms with a hint of green at their heart. Its perfect geometry, with not a petal out of place, is reminiscent of the stylised portrayals of flowers in the pages of Elizabethan herbals. In fact, *Ranunculus aconitifolius* 'Flore Pleno' (d) was recorded in *Gerard's Herbal*, first published in 1597. It seems to have no particular medicinal use. Presumably it was grown then as it is now – purely for its aesthetic worth.

Which is the most beautiful? Opinions vary, sometimes diametrically. Reginald Farrer in *The English Rock Garden* extols the single, calling it 'that noble fairy', whilst denigrating the double. Christopher Lloyd finds the double 'a scintillating plant' but thinks the single 'scarcely deserving of garden space'. Personally I welcome them both. The plants that is, not the men, would I should be so lucky – but wouldn't it be entertaining to have their company in the garden at the same time!

Despite being a tough bunch, Cinderellas often fall foul of over-zealous gardeners. Because of their early hibernation they are invisible for most of the year. It is too easy to go in with the trowel and a cavalier attitude when you spy a bare patch of earth and need to find a home for some newly acquired treasure. I have done it time and again with my favourite Cinderella, *Ranunculus aconitifolius*. To dwell on how easy it is to lose this plant seems a bit off-putting but, providing you manage to hang on to it, the enjoyment it offers when at its peak is second to none.

Ranunculus acris 'Citrinus' is essentially a plant of damp fields, a version of our native meadow buttercup. It has the same wiry, branching stems awash with simple flowers. Its pale-lemon petals are just as polished as the wild plant, on sunny days reflecting the blue sky and bringing it down to ground level. Individual flowers may not last long, but they are borne in succession from late April through to July. Often the foliage has marked chocolatey splodges – a lovely feature when the spring garden is still at the leafy stage.

Several marginal bog plants are perfectly at home away from the water's edge, providing they have heavy damp soil in shade. *Caltha palustris*, marsh marigolds or kingcups, make one of the brightest contributions to countryside ponds and damp woodland, and are equally welcome in our gardens. Big, kidney-shaped leaves and fleshy stems make a luscious background for the large chrome-yellow cups which open from fat round buds. There is a double form and a white single. Both are lovely but neither can compare to the undiluted ebullience of the kingcup.

Globeflowers will flower to perfection in wet soil and seem oblivious of light levels. Our native, *Trollius europaeus*, is a lovely plant – its pale-lemon globes perfectly complemented in the garden by the purple flowers of *Geranium sylvaticum*, a combination still seen in the wild, especially in the north. *Trollius chinensis* 'Golden Queen' is a showier plant. Not only is it bigger, in damp soil it will reach two feet plus, but its colour is more striking, some would say brash. I love its huge, orange-yellow globes with their equally vivid stamens bursting through.

Occasionally when I am bemoaning my heavy soil I stop for a moment. I consider how lucky we are here, and how we should spare a thought for all those on light, thin soils with perfect drainage, who will never know the joy of growing buttercups.

OPPOSITE
Nature's flower arrangement, meadow buttercups, sorrel and grasses.

Foxgloves

Foxgloves are instantly recognisable. The long, purple-pink bells of our native foxglove, *Digitalis purpurea*, with its characteristic spotted throats, are an iconic image. It's one that can be summoned up by gardeners and non-gardeners alike, and we all see it with a big fat bumble bee buzzing in and out collecting nectar and pollen.

Whenever plantations of conifers are felled for timber on tracts of Forestry Commission land close to us, the ground around them appears barren for a year. But in the next season the hillside is awash with a pink sea, full of the tall, distinctive spires of foxgloves. As light and rain at last penetrate the earth, the seed bank that has lain dormant in the surrounding soil erupts into growth. There is something magical about the way these tall spires appear from nowhere.

This is a wild flower that no one can ignore, sometimes growing as tall as a tall man and much, much taller than me. Sometimes it's good being short, and in this case those of us who

are vertically challenged can look up into the foxglove bells and view the secrets inside with ease.

D. purpurea is a biennial and sets copious amounts of seed. In a garden situation it needs to be planted in two consecutive years so that new plants and flowers will be produced every year. The white-flowered variety, *D. purpurea* f. *albiflora*, is a lovely plant and looks particularly good in the shady corners where it most likes to grow. Give it a soil rich in humus and it will grow happily, eventually making good colonies, providing the seedheads are left to throw their seed around.

One of the most awkward situations in any garden is its edges, whether its boundaries are hedges, walls or fences. The plants that grow with them as a backdrop need to be extra accommodating, able to contend with uneven light, sometimes bright and baking, at other times plunged into shade and with erratic amounts of water. Foxgloves are more than up to the job, simply because they thrive in the wild in exactly the same conditions – they are archetypal hedgerow plants. Hedges aren't a natural phenomenon, they are man-made, but plants such as *Euphorbia amygdaloides*, the wood spurge, and our wild primrose have successfully made the transition from their natural habitat, the woodland edge, to the hedgerow.

ABOVE
Foxgloves often seed themselves.

OPPOSITE
Their spires of purple bells are iconic.

Cultivated cousins

Whilst our native foxglove is a biennial, there is a whole clan of perennial, albeit short-lived, foxgloves from the European mainland. Most are perfectly hardy, though they are liable to need more sun than in their native habitats to compensate for lower temperatures. Though many would grow in partial shade 'at home' most are happy out in the open garden here. They have been much used in recent years by innovative designers alongside grasses and umbels.

Pale-flowered foxgloves are particularly easy to incorporate in any colour scheme. *D. lutea* has small, fine and creamy coloured bells on stems between 45cm (18in) and 60cm (2ft) tall. It may keep going for a few years. *D. grandiflora*, which used to be known as *D. ambigua*, is a lovely plant with large cream bells. It makes a real clump and produces stem after stem of flower. It can live for many years. Try it close to the glossy leaves of *Acanthus mollis* or associate it with *Baptisia australis*, agapanthus or blue aconites. It is also perfect set against Bowles's golden grass, *Milium effusum* 'Aureum'.

The rusty foxglove, *D. ferruginea*, goes with everything. Its flowers, small and hooded, are a bizarre mixture of browns, creams and yellows and they thickly clothe the stout stems. Even more unusual, *D. parviflora* has tiny rich-brown flowers held tightly side by side. Both the inflorescence and the stem are covered in fine soft fluff. This foxglove creates a small landing stage at the entrance to each flower on which small bees and other pollinating insects can land. Immediately inside the bell of the flower are two bright yellow anthers, bristling with pollen with which any prospective pollinator is anointed. The seedheads that follow are remarkable. Firstly they are thick and full, crowding the stems, and each seedpod is barbed at one end, presumably to put off grazing animals in their native Spain and Portugal. They are tough, too, and almost impossible to penetrate. When saving seed, even though the seedpods are fully developed and the seed is ripe, you sometimes have to crush the pods slightly to extract the seed. Secondly, the stems are straight as a dye. These bronze ramrods, which last all winter through, make the perfect punctuation to a narrow herbaceous bed where there is no room for a fastigiate shrub. Its colouring and deportment make this a very beautiful plant, rather odd, but very desirable.

D. × mertonensis is another one-off. Bred at the John Innes Centre, it had artificial colouring introduced into its genes, giving it a most unusual colour – its broad, squashed bells have a delightful strawberry, raspberry smoothie kind of colour.

OPPOSITE TOP LEFT
Straight as a ramrod, *Digitalis ferruginea*.
TOP RIGHT
White foxgloves are especially enchanting.

BELOW LEFT
Furry and fun, *Digitalis parviflora*.
BELOW RIGHT
Squashed bells of crushed strawberry, *Digitalis × mertonensis*.

The shrubby evergreen foxglove, *D. canariensis*, is unique. Although it is somewhat tender, most of us would be prepared to go to great trouble to protect it each winter just to get an annual view of its rich, amber-chestnut bell flowers. This is a plant which merits a place on its own as a specimen plant, and some gardeners grow it in a pot in loam-based compost, taking it outside for the summer season and returning it to a cold greenhouse when temperatures drop.

The rest of the bunch probably look at their best growing together with others of their ilk – in a mixed planting with other woodland subjects or, for the Southern European species, flowering alongside *Scabiosa columbaria* subsp. *ochroleuca* or the dramatic *S. atropurpurea* in a sunny site. Close your eyes and you can almost hear the bees buzzing.

Any foxglove will come true to its species from seed, although seed from *D. purpurea* f. *albiflora* is not guaranteed to yield white-flowered plants. Collect seed when the capsules have turned brown and are just about to burst. One capsule may provide as many as 100 seeds. Put the ripe seedhead into a paper bag and hang in a cool, dry place until it has opened and shed its seeds.

Seed can be separated and stored in envelopes until needed (the best place is in the fridge but any cool place will do), or it can be sown immediately. Fill a half seed tray with any good seed compost, strike off and press lightly with a piece of board or another seed tray. Sow the seed on the surface of the compost and cover with sharp grit. Firm once more then stand the whole seed tray in shallow water until the grit looks damp. Take out, drain, and place in a cold frame or greenhouse shelf out of direct sunlight.

Germination of fresh seed is usually fairly rapid. Once seedlings have developed true leaves they can be pricked out individually into cell trays or small pots. Pot on into bigger pots and plant out either that autumn or in early spring in the following year. Foxgloves always look best in swathes or waves, which emulate the way they occur naturally.

OPPOSITE TOP LEFT
Apricot foxgloves and silvery cat.
TOP RIGHT
Testing the seedpods – nearly ready.

OPPOSITE BELOW
Raising plants from seed means you can make a real show.

Poppies

The field, or corn, poppy, *Papaver rhoeas*, is older than mankind and we have a long and intimate relationship with it. Our shared story is interwoven with one of our most fundamental needs – the necessity to eat bread and grow cereals to make it. Poppies must have been around long before the human race burst upon the scene, and since the dawn of civilization, and our first rudimentary attempts at agriculture, it has grown amongst the corn we cultivate to make our daily bread. Poppies are persistent. Poppy seed can live for hundreds of years. Germination often follows the ground being disturbed. The corn poppy is the most obvious illustration, a new generation germinating each year as the land was ploughed and the grain scattered. This is our 'Remembrance Day' poppy, which so poignantly regenerates on the old battle sites of Flanders Fields. It's a significant plant in many cultures – for the Ancient Egyptians it symbolised blood and rebirth, and the Romans venerated it as the sacred crop of Ceres. Poppies represent a metaphor for the earth's fecundity and human fertility.

There is poetry in its being so tough, so irrepressible and yet seeming so fragile. John Ruskin, in *Proserpina* (1875–1886), his study of wayside flowers, wrote: 'We usually think of the poppy as a coarse flower: but it is the most transparent and delicate of all the blossoms of the field. The rest – nearly all of them – depend on the texture of their surfaces for colour. But the poppy is painted glass; it never glows so brightly as when the sun shines through it. Wherever it is seen – against the light or with the light – always, it is a flame and warms the wind like a blown ruby ... Gather a green poppy bud, just when it shows the scarlet line at its side; break it open and unpack the poppy. The whole flower is there complete in size and colour – the stamens full-grown, but all packed so closely that the fine silk of the petals is crushed into millions of shapeless wrinkles. When the flower opens, it seems a deliverance from torture.' For human beings the poppy has always had a dual symbolism, that of life and death, of eternal youth and inevitable mortality.

Cultivated cousins

The plant family, papaveraceae, is relatively small, with less than 800 species (yes, that's small). Though poppies must be amongst the most ephemeral of blooms, they imprint their image on our minds more strongly than almost any other flower. From the fields of the Somme turned blood red with the massed blooms of *P. rhoeas*, to the equally red and even more demonstrative flowers of *P. orientale* Goliath Group on shoulder-high stems, poppies are never ignored, they always get noticed.

The petals of all their flowers may share the same tissue-paper quality, yet the plants

themselves range from indestructible perennials to flash-in-the-pan annuals. There are also tiny, ground-hugging alpines, like *P. miyabeanum*, those with tall spires, like *P. pilosum* subsp. *spicatum* dressed in fat buds and covered in silvery fur, or the even more statuesque stems of *Macleaya cordata*, the plume poppy. The emerging leaves of macleaya, in their colour, form and the way they emerge from the soil in pairs, closely resemble Blood Root, *Sanguinaria canadensis*. It's a woodland wonder from eastern North America, and the only sanguinaria within the papaveraceae family. The whole plant, including the thick, spreading rootstock that bleeds red sap when damaged, is succulent and fleshy. Each emerging flower bud is wrapped tightly in one scalloped leaf, which unfurls as the flower stem pushes up its fragile flower. The simple, pure-white flowers are fleeting, almost ghostly in their transparence, seldom lasting more than a day or two – a mere nuance of a flower.

The double form, *S. canadensis* f. *multiplex* (d) is longer lasting and more often cultivated. Its chunky, globose flowers are laden generously with pristine petals, in telling contrast to the puckered grey of its protecting leaf. Once seen, never forgotten.

In the main, poppies are sun-lovers, but there are several amongst the meconopsis arm of the family that are more at home in the dappled shade beneath deciduous trees. Our own Welsh poppy, *Meconopsis cambrica*, frequents stretches of woodland, throwing seeds around and colonising ground between bluebells and wood anemones. Usually yellow-flowered, occasionally they are orange and rarely red. Although the wilding is single with papery petals and a boss of quivering golden anthers, there are double-flowered cultivars too – they're more showy but lack the grace of the simple single.

Blue flowers are always a draw but none have such magnetism as those whose colour reminds us of the sea and the sky. The blue Himalayan poppy, *M. betonicifolia*, is an ooh-aah plant. Looking into an individual flower is a revelation. Each deep caerulean-blue and slightly crumpled petal is elegantly poised. As the flower opens fully the petals are stretched smooth like wet silk drying on a hot day. At the centre of their shallow cups, a boss of fine stamens. Their anthers, dusted in gold, surround the central stigma which thrusts itself forward, intent on pollination. The elegant foliage, the stems and the drooping, dimpled buds are all covered in a fine bronze fuzz designed to catch every drop of dew on the high eastern slopes of its homeland.

Meconopsis do best where the climate is closest to their natural environment – cool and

OPPOSITE TOP LEFT
Meconopsis grandis.
Everyone wants to grow the blue Himalayan poppy.
TOP RIGHT
Most of us would find the Welsh poppy, *Meconopsis cambrica,* an easier proposition and just as beautiful.

BELOW LEFT
Biggest and brightest, first prize to *Papaver orientale* 'Beauty of Livermere'.
BELOW RIGHT
P. orientale 'Patty's Plum', dark and luscious.

moist. High humidity and rich soil are what they need. *M. betonicifolia* is short-lived, often monocarpic, whereas *M. grandis* is a perennial but loathe to set seed. A newly introduced strain, *M.meconopsis* 'Lingholm', produces viable seed and is fairly easy to raise. Because poppy seed is always very fine it's tempting to sow it thickly. In the event most seed germinates but it often collapses due to damping off – a fungal disease that attacks seedlings. It's always better to sow thinly.

Blue meconopsis enjoy shade but the great majority of poppies thrive in the open garden. Of these the most familiar, and by far the most ostentatious, is *Papaver orientale*. When it was given its 'orientale', the orient was the Middle East as that was as far as we'd got. The antecedents of this plant inhabit Turkish hillsides in full sun. Its flowers are bold but fleeting. Sometimes it feels as though getting there at dawn is the only way to ensure witnessing *P. orientale* in our gardens in its full glory. Well worth getting up early, and maybe staying for the day, to see the buds burst, their coverings fall and the petals stretch – free at last.

There are so many *P. orientale* from which to choose. Dark and dramatic? 'Patty's Plum' fits the bill. Pretty in pink 'Karine' has flowers of soft rose and a daintiness about its neat petals. New varieties with stronger stems, unusual petal shapes and distinctive colours are constantly introduced. 'Earl Grey', 'Manhattan' and 'Sunset' are relatively recent introductions, but each year there are more and more, including a group of so-called 'Super Poppies' which are purportedly

more robust and longer flowering. Most named oriental poppies are sterile, and best propagated by root cuttings. Most species poppies rely on seed to keep them going.

P. somniferum, the opium poppy, is a crop itself in some parts of the world. In our gardens it is appreciated for its ornamental value. At a rapid (some would say alarming) pace, its stout stems shoot up, wrapped with wavy-edged, glaucous leaves and lateral shoots all terminating in plump, dimpled buds. At this stage there are waves of excitement to see what colour and form the flowers will have when the buds finally burst. Even when there is only one poppy in the garden, its progeny can be completely different from one another and from their mother. There are reds, pinks and purples, black and white. Some are single and elegant, some as fussy and frilly as a Barbara Cartland blouse. They are all followed by round pepper-pot seedpods, immensely decorative in their own right.

Poppies of every description are always welcome in our gardens.

OPPOSITE
Papaver somniferum is a prolific self-seeder. It's good to save some too so you can have them where you want them!

Cranesbills

Driving along country roads at midsummer your eyes seem sometimes to deceive you. The verdant green of the grass changes from time to time with a pure blue that mingles with it, giving it a new depth. The effect is created by the flowers of *Geranium pratense* – the meadow cranesbill. They cast a haze of blue, and should you get the opportunity to stop and meet them face to face you will encounter one of the most gracious and endearing of all our wild flowers.

When hay meadows were a feature of the rural scene, these blue flowers must have graced them, growing up amongst a melée of other wild flowers and a plethora of grasses. Changes in agricultural practice saw its exile to road verges and hedgerows, but this is a plant with a lust for life. Where the importance of allowing wild flowers to do their thing is recognised, it has been able to adapt to pastures new, or at least to road verges new. It is a short-lived perennial, but its substantial seeds are catapulted hither and thither meaning that eventually it makes

colonies, spreading itself through the grass. It is a poetic flower with a raggle-taggle romance of its own.

Its petals are muslin-thin and translucent, and with the sunlight streaming through them all the delicate veins that decorate them are highlighted. If you look at the back of the flowers, the opened calyx that once covered their buds stretches itself out like a star supporting the petals. These ephemeral, chalice-shaped flowers last no longer than a few days, but there are many of them held on branching stems, and as the confetti petals fall they are replaced by the seedheads that give the plant its popular name. *Geranos* is the Greek for crane, and it is easy to see when you study the seed capsule just why it is so called. At the base of the long beak, the seeds are clustered each with its own spring that reaches the tip of the beak. As they ripen and swell the spring coils tightly, and rapidly launches the seeds into the air.

We have other indigenous cranesbills. *G. sylvaticum*, with flowers of pale purple, is a handsome plant flowering in late May alongside trollius, the globe flower whose lemon colour is the perfect complement. This couple is more often seen in the north growing in damp places, along riverbanks or where an underground stream lies just below the surface of a Scottish hillside.

ABOVE
Taking a really close look.
OPPOSITE
The transluscence of the

petals of *Geranium pratense* focuses the interest of pollinating insects on the treats to be had.

The pretty little herb robert, *G. robertianum*, with rubescent foliage, dainty pink flowers and a characteristic aroma, is an endearing plant. Sometimes you smell it as you weed it out, sometimes you don't weed it out because it always seems to put itself in just the right place, and looks so happy with its perfectly symmetrical rosette of deeply cut leaves.

Cultivated cousins

What do you do with the large blank space in the middle of the border? The big arid patch on top of a wall? The dark and dingy area under the canopy of overhanging trees where nothing seems to grow? If there is one genus of plants that provides the answer to these, and countless other gardening conundrums, it is the cranesbill family. As Margery Fish, the doyenne of cottage gardening would say, 'If in doubt – plant a geranium.'

Once vaguely unfashionable, and used mainly for infill between more self-important plants, hardy geraniums are enjoying a revival. With the vogue for easy-going plants that excel without pampering or preening, geraniums are now at the forefront of the 21st-Century Garden.

OPPOSITE ABOVE
Geranium phaeum – best friends with *Chaerophyllum hirsutum* 'Roseum'.
BELOW
Geranium wallichianum 'Buxton's Blue' mingles perfectly with a good blue form of *Eryngium bourgatii*.

Coming from a variety of habitats and from all over the Northern Hemisphere, there are geraniums for every sort of situation. To choose the right cranesbill for a specific site, find out about its genealogy.

G. sanguineum var. *striatum* used to be *G. sanguineum* 'Lancastriense'. It comes from Walney Island off the Lancashire coast, so it's a racing certainty that it will do well in light soil, tolerate high exposure and luxuriate in full light. We were lucky enough to visit Walney Island with the programme, and to see it for ourselves growing on the edge of the dunes alongside its more predominant counterpart, the vivid-magenta *G. sanguineum*. Low mats of close foliage are spangled with pale-pink flowers etched with deeper-pink lines. It flowers all summer long.

G. sanguineum, known as the bloody cranesbill (probably because of its rubescent autumn foliage rather than its bad habits), is an ideal candidate for a gravel garden or the front of a sun-drenched border. If you are not into pink there is a lovely white-flowered form, *G. sanguineum* 'Album', with wiry stems and informal flowers, and there are also any number of cultivars and selections with intense magenta flowers.

Plunging into the shadows, most shade-loving cranesbills such as *G. sylvaticum*, *G. phaeum* and *G. maculatum* flower in the spring, exploiting the light before the tree canopy fills in overhead. But one, *G. nodosum*, can be relied upon to brighten up the darkest corners from May till November. In autumn, neat clumps of evergreen foliage are set aflame, becoming bronze and orange. The flowers are lilac, but I have one called *G. nodosum* 'Dark Heart' with deep-purple, velvety flowers. Watch out though, *G. nodosum* is a tenacious plant, no respecter of boundaries – Christopher Lloyd waged war on it.

For the open border, *G.* × *oxonianum* is virtually indestructible, making low mats thick with flowers. If it gets out of hand after midsummer, shear it back hard – it will be in flower again within weeks.

First prize for the most upbeat, and most delectable, of all cranesbills goes to *G. psilostemon*. It will grow anywhere for anybody. Its tall stature and vivid magenta flowers, with their captivating black centres, make it everyone's favourite. *G. psilostemon* must have featured on more '10 best plants' lists than any other herbaceous perennial. With its big, bold structure, and its wealth of flowers, it is not a plant for the faint-hearted. It has been in cultivation here for well over a century and used to be known as *G. armenum*. It is widespread in northern Turkey and the Caucasus, growing in mountain meadows alongside other big herbaceous plants and grasses. Not suprisingly these are exactly the conditions it enjoys in our gardens. It is a neighbourly, mingling sort of a plant, although it should always be given enough room to be itself. *G. psilostemon* is perhaps my all-time favourite – if you don't already grow it, try it. Even if you have no garden it is worth planting in a big container of loam-based compost. Like so many cranesbills it has fibrous roots and will live happily in such a situation.

Several cranesbills don't begin their best show until autumn takes over, exhibiting a fine palette of reds, oranges and russets in their foliage, often accompanied by their flowers. The foliage of *G. wallichianum* 'Buxton's Variety' turns vivid-red and the sprawling stems, ideal for tumbling down a shady bank, are spangled with vivid-blue flowers with a distinctive white centre. Hybridists have used it to produce several cultivars – *G. Rozanne* is a compact selection and flowers all summer and autumn long. Try it in a container out of the sun with large-leaved hostas, ferns or a dark-leaved rodgersia. Non-stop flowers.

I make no apologies for my love of cranesbills, we use them shamelessly at Glebe Cottage and the garden would be bereft without them.

Roses

As I left home for Dutton Hall in Lancashire to join our crew and film the Roses sequence for *Gardeners' World*, the hedges in Devon were still festooned with the pink and white flowers of *Rosa canina*. Its great thorny stems were ambling along the hedges and hoisting themselves into holly and hawthorn. At Dutton, though, the flowers were on the wane but, down at the bottom of the fields adjoining the garden where we were filming, we found a magnificent old briar with white flowers still going strong. As the sun began to climb, the air was alive with insects, many of them attracted by the fragrance of the rose, no doubt looking for pollen. It's a feast for them, and for the honey bees – the vital ingredient for the next generation. Pollen is packed with protein and this is what the young grubs feed on.

Typically *R. canina* flowers have five petals, each separate and tapering towards the base. There are always lots of stamens arranged in a circle, giving an almost powder-puff effect inside the flower. At their base is the hypanthium, which encloses the ovary. This is the bit that, after pollination, swells and becomes the fruit enclosing the seeds – the rose hip. The sepals that form the outside protective layer of the bud open wide to form a platform for the petals. They persist at the tip of each rose hip as those hips develop.

All our wild roses bar one – *R. spinosissima*, whose fruit are black – have orangey-red hips. They are a vital food source for resident birds and for winter visitors, redwings and fieldfares, en route from their summer nesting grounds in Scandinavia. They have been, and still are, used medicinally and in jams, jellies and cordials as they're packed full of vitamin C, so full in fact that during World War Two they became an essential source to compensate for the lack of citric fruit when convoys carrying it were attacked by German submarines.

The dog rose is our national flower, yet of all the roses so often used here in heraldry, and depicted in art from tapestries, paintings to wood carvings in churches or stately homes, none is a wild rose. Roses have been in cultivation here for many centuries and longer still in the Middle East. They were often brought back from crusades and trading expeditions, and these cultivated roses upstaged our own wild rose, relegating it to the most

ABOVE
The magnificent hips of *Rosa rugosa* 'Scabrosa'!

OPPOSITE
Although *Rosa rugosa* doesn't belong here, there's no choice than to revel in its beauty.

base position – hence the prefix 'dog', given to any flower considered too common for further consideration. There are numerous references to cultivated roses in Shakespeare's plays and sonnets but, unusually for that time, he reveres wild roses in *A Midsummer Night's Dream*.

R. canina is the most widespread and commonly encountered of our wild roses. *R. arvensis*, the field rose, is very similar though tends to be more dense in habit and seldom scrambles more than a couple of yards high. It is most common in the southern half of the British Isles and Ireland. The burnet rose, *R. pimpinellifolia*, is a suckering shrub often growing in sandy or chalky soils. Though it is low to the ground, seldom higher than a yard, it makes dense thickets and spreads extensively in the light soils it relishes. Its flowers are creamy white and have the most exquisite scent of all our roses – that's saying something. Perhaps to ensure adequate pollination in the kind of areas it grows, often very exposed and many of them close to the sea, it needs a powerful perfume. We met it on our visit to Walney Island, scrambling around amongst marram grass at the back of the dunes.

Another seaside rose that has become a feature of many coastal areas is *R. rugosa*.

It is not a native and hails from coastal areas of Japan, Korea, China and Siberia. Used originally as a hedging rose, it has made itself happily at home and is a delight with bright apple-green leaves that turn to amber in the autumn, huge magenta flowers and big flagon-shaped hips of sealing-wax red. Perhaps not *comme il faut* on a British beach, but in our gardens *R. rugosa* is an invaluable plant.

Cultivated cousins

Not so long ago, any garden that did not have roses as a central component in its planting schemes would have been deemed unworthy of the name. Fashions change and in more recent years the rose has fallen out of favour. Christopher Lloyd was one of the first to reject the holy cow, ripping out the old, tired formal rose garden at Great Dixter (designed by none less than Lutyens) and replacing it with the Exotic Garden. It is a triumph of showy tender perennials, many of statuesque proportions and vibrant colour.

There is no place in prairie planting for roses, especially not of the ilk of hybrid teas or floribundas. And yet Graham Stuart Thomas, the great rosarian and plantsman with his redesign of Mottisfont Abbey's Rose Garden, demonstrated how perfectly to blend shrub roses with herbaceous perennials. Here, his collections of old roses were planted alongside scabious and astrantia, stachys and artemisia, emulating the way nature combines such plants. He brought them together where they can still be seen, not in a museum context but as a joyous

OPPOSITE ABOVE
Both the hips and the flowers of our most familiar wild rose, *Rosa canina*, are vital sources of food for wildlife and a constant source of pleasure for us.

OPPOSITE BELOW
From the wild to the height of cultivation, cascades of *Rosa* 'Adélaïde d'Orléans' at Mottisfont Abbey.

display of living, growing plants. In nature roses would grow amongst other plants, wild flowers and grasses. The roses, many of them rescued from obscurity, some on the point of extinction, are happy and healthy.

In the 'average' garden there is plenty of scope to include a few shrub roses. Well-chosen, they will fit in with herbaceous perennials, shrubs and climbers in a happy homogeny. Which roses to choose, though? The selection is bewildering. The qualities we need are universally agreed – good health, vigour, disease resistance (especially important when gardening organically), glossy foliage and large quantities of beautiful, fragrant flowers which last well. Repeat flowering is an added bonus.

There are two major groups from which to choose – the old roses and the modern shrub roses, many of which have been developed from the old roses. Of the old roses, the three subgroups with the most going for them are the Alba roses, the Gallicas and the Damasks. The Albas make big bushes with glorious glaucous leaves, seldom affected by mildew or black spot. The handsome foliage makes a fine foil for the refined buds and flowers; almost all are white, although a few are pale pink, including my favourite, R. 'Céleste', which when it is half-open is the most perfect rose ever. The great double White or Jacobite rose is still found in many old gardens. It makes a large shrub, up to 1.8m (6ft), smothered for much of the summer with large, double, white flowers.

The Damask roses are often pale-flowered although they are very variable and include a few bright-pink and even magenta flowers. Their foliage is downy and their stems thorny. Attar of roses is derived from R. damascena. R. 'Madame Hardy' is one of the most outstanding damasks with white, full-petalled flat flowers with a green eye.

The gallica rose is embodied by R. 'Charles de Mills', a crimson rose with perfect form and heavenly scent.

Modern shrub roses are personified in the English roses developed by David Austin. They marry the best of both worlds – the charm, scent and character of the old roses with the repeat flowering, disease resistance and kaleidoscopic colour range of modern roses. From R. William Shakespeare in rich crimson to R. The Shepherdess in soft apricot pink, they are carefree and rewarding plants.

OPPOSITE TOP LEFT
Rosa 'Madame Isaac Pereire' mingles with the peach-leafed bellflower.
TOP RIGHT
The buds of moss rose *Rosa* 'William Lobb' are fragrant.
BELOW LEFT
Rosa 'Little White Pet' has a glorious musky fragrance.
BELOW RIGHT
Rosa 'Rosa Mundi' in our daughter Alice's garden. Her second name is Rosamund.

Umbels

For 15 years my nursery, Glebe Cottage Plants, exhibited at the RHS Chelsea Flower Show. Every year as our lorry turned from Pixie Lane at the start of the journey, the ditches and verges effervesced with cow parsley – wave after wave of it rolling along the hedgerows, and forcing even dark corners to join in the spumy celebration. Although this is the opening act of the umbel drama, there will be members of the family carrying the torch throughout late spring, into summer and beyond – hogweed, hemlock and wild carrot adorning road verge and field edge, waste ground and cliff edge.

Cow parsley, or *Anthriscus sylvestris*, has a host of common names – a sure sign of the fondness in which it is held. Queen Anne's Lace is another popular epithet, and perfectly describes the delicacy of the dainty flowers that make up each flower head in their hundreds. This construction is typical of most umbels, sometimes composed of 'umbellets' or 'umbellules' – umbels of umbels. It is a form that gives members of this part of the family, especially those with white flowers, a lightness and grace unmatched in any other plant family (some have yellow flowers and occasionally they may be pink).

Most umbellifers have intricately detailed flowers. They can be seen on many levels, becoming increasingly more complex as our eyes move in – like a selection of frames from a movie, they yield different realities within the same head of flower. From a distance cow parsley makes a fine, frothy picture, full of creamy softness. Closer up, with the whole flowerhead in frame, we are aware of its structure, of the individual stems all emanating in a starburst from the summit of the main stem, and each supporting its own smaller umbel of flowers. We can move closer again to study each perfect flower.

Walk past any umbel on a sunny day and it will be teeming with insects. Although some insects have an umbel of choice, most seem to have catholic tastes and at any one time there may be numerous species of flies, hoverflies and bees as well as a collection of beetles. Wasps seem to be partial to angelicas, particularly *Angelica gigas* with its magnificent platforms of brooding, crimson flowers. Don't be put

ABOVE
It's worth perusing umbels at close quarters to appreciate their geometry.
OPPOSITE
Nothing is so fulsome or so frothy as cow parsley.

off, though, wasps do an enormous amount of good, especially when it comes to hoovering up caterpillars – they're always welcome on my cabbages. Hoverfly larvae consume aphis by the hundreds, so apiaceae are good news all round.

Cow parsley grows profusely where we live, but we seldom see wild carrot, *Daucus carota* – it prefers lighter soil than ours and good drainage. It is widespread, though, one of its favourite haunts being seaside venues and chalky downland. Taking photos for this book, Jonathan and I met it on Braunton Burrows growing in the sand and at the edge of the slacks beyond.

Though I'm not keen on motorway travel, stopping at service stations in spring and summer is an unexpected opportunity to come face-to-face with wild flowers. Many, including *Daucus carota*, thrive in the untended environs of slip roads and car parks. For the programme we saw it at Marchants Hardy Plants in East Sussex. Their garden is anything but unkempt – it is staggeringly beautiful and in a couple of areas the wild flora, including lovely colonies of wild carrot, are encouraged to do their thing.

Cultivated cousins

Few of us have the space to give cow parsley garden room. Its bronze-leaved twin, *A. sylvestris* 'Ravenswing', though, is welcome in polite society. Its flowers are as attractive as those of the species, and tinged with pink to boot, but it is its ferny, burnt-sienna foliage that tempts the gardener to invite it in.

Several other umbels make alluring additions to informal areas, and bring the ebullient spirit of cow parsley into the garden. *Chaerophyllum hirsutum* 'Roseum' is more reserved at first – initially its soft, ferny leaves are almost sessile (attached directly to the base). Its flower stems and buds lie along the surface of the soil as though too shy to show themselves, and looking like some newborn creature. In its own time it lifts itself up and proceeds to branch and fill out, blossoming into a plant 1m (40in) high and smothered in myriad tiny purple-pink flowers. Grow it in light shade among Solomon's seal, or rising from a sea of lily-of-the-valley. *Hirsutum* means hairy, and the whole plant is soft to the touch.

Pimpinella major 'Rosea' has similar flowers. It is daintier than chaerophyllum, and is the pink version of a British native, the greater burnet saxifrage. Its foliage is more succulent than cow parsley's, and the whole plant is more erect and compact than its hedge-hugging relative. Its immensely pretty flowers are a lovely shade of pink with no blue in it – they make a perfect foil for the big, blowsy poppies that are at their best in the early days of June. Try it with the shell-pink blooms of *Papaver*

OPPOSITE TOP LEFT
The pale, dainty flowers of *Anthriscus sylvestris* 'Ravenswing' contrast perfectly with its dark, ferny leaves.
TOP RIGHT
Astrantia 'Roma', clear pink flowers surrounded by papery bracts.

BELOW LEFT
For drama and impact nothing could beat *Angelica gigas*.
BELOW RIGHT
And nothing could compare with the delicacy of *Orlaya grandiflora*.

orientale 'Karine', or set it against the dark, opulent discs of *P. orientale* 'Patty's Plum'.

In the north of the country, and especially in parts of Scotland, one of the most endearing of umbels holds sway. *Meum athamanticum* (hasn't it got a lovely ring to it?) has pretty flowers, but it is its foliage that pulls in the crowds. At Chelsea Flower Show it was almost impossible to stop visitors stroking its immensely soft leaves, so finely cut as to be almost fluffy – you can see its close family resemblance to dill, my favourite herb. Its common names are Spignel and Baldmoney, the latter from an ancient Nordic god, Baldr, who was associated with light and beauty. It used to be cultivated as a root crop in Scotland.

Selinum wallichianum is always extolled by celebrated gardeners, often featuring in their lists of 'top ten' perennials. Early in the year its lacy leaves make great rosettes like huge green doilies nestling on the ground. By late summer its towering stems, clothed in the same ferny leaves, push through. It reaches its peak in late summer, opening its heads of white flowers. Each year it gains in stature and is long-lived and enduring. So too is *Athamanta turbith* (candy carrot) – a plant or two of this looks like a green mist with white clouds suspended in its midst.

At the other end of the longevity scale, but equally beautiful, are plants such as *Ammi majus* and *Orlaya grandiflora*. Flower arrangers love *A. majus*, or common bishop's weed, as it brings a touch of levity to more substantial blooms. It serves the same purpose in the garden, as does *O. grandiflora* whose platform of tiny flowers is encircled by larger, sterile flowers, making it especially exquisite. Both are easy to raise from seed. Once you have grown orlaya you need its company year after year. The archetypal mingler, it never looks out of place and adds light and buoyancy to heavy planting schemes. It reaches 55cm (22in) tall.

Angelica archangelica can be used as a specimen plant. It can reach 1.2–1.5m (4–5ft) high with bold, shiny green leaves and saucers of lime-green flowers. *Angelica gigas*, from the Far East, looks quite ordinary in its early stages but is transformed as its flower stems shoot up, into a tumult of crimson. *Angelica atropurpurea* has dark, purple-red stems and white flowerheads.

At first glimpse there is little family resemblance between astrantias and the typical umbels, with their flat heads composed of myriad flowers. On closer inspection, the same tiny flowers can be seen dancing on the end of fine filaments, the whole bouquet surrounded by papery bracts. This construction gives the plant one of its country names, 'Hattie's pincushion'. As flowers turn to seed, the papery skirt maintains its attraction, sometimes for months, making astrantias one of the most

OPPOSITE TOP
Flowers within flowers within flowers. *Chaerophyllum hirsutum* 'Roseum'.
BELOW
Collecting seed from *Anthriscus sylvestris* 'Ravenswing', some to sow fresh, some for next spring.

valuable of all herbaceous perennials.

One of the most subtle is the species plant *Astrantia major*, or as its country name would have it 'melancholy gentleman' – it's a quiet study in green and white. The astrantias that have taken centre stage over the last 20 years are those with rich crimson bracts. There are numerous selections, from *A.* 'Hadspen Blood' to *A. major* 'Ruby Wedding'. Finally there is *Astrantia* 'Roma', a very notable cross between *A. major* and *A. maxima*, which inherits the latter's pink bracts and flowers. 'Roma' is one of the best introductions of the last decade and since it is sterile, seems to maintain its show longer.

This year, 2012, the plants of *A.* 'Roma' that we've included in our new raised beds in the bottom half of the garden have been exceptional. Normally, though its flowers last long, there comes a point when they must be removed – that is it then for the rest of the season. But our plants here not only made a magnificent display in the first part of the year, but have put on a second show easily the equal of the first.

Sea hollies (eryngiums) are another part of the same genus that does not quite fit the family profile. Like the astrantias they guard their flowers with a circle of bracts, but this time they are armed and dangerous. The bracts of European sea hollies are sharp and barbed, in

some cases brutal, but they protect the central flower cone, and later its seeds, from predation.

Umbels are basically carrots and as such, with the possible exception of astrantias, all have tap roots and cannot be divided. Seed is easy to collect, and the best policy is to sow some straight away and save some for the following spring.

OPPOSITE
Two days after Jonathan took this picture, this marsh dropwort was cut to the ground.

ABOVE
As its first umbels open fully, *Daucus carota* is at its best, though it will continue its show for many weeks.

Daisies

There is a bit of a competition about which plant family is the largest but, when it comes to flowering plants, the daisy family, asteraceae, wins hands down with a staggering 22,750-plus species. Members of the family inhabit every part of the world with the exception of Antarctica. One in 10 of all the flowers on the planet belong to this genus, and their range stretches from the tropics to the arctic regions. There are daisies that thrive in hot sun on mountainsides, and those that luxuriate in boggy conditions. Presumably they owe their huge diversity to being able to evolve and adapt over millennia to all manner of conditions.

The old name for the family was compositae, and that gives us a clue to one of the common features shared by members of the family. Instead of having single flowers, each 'flowerhead' is composed of many flowers. Look at a dandelion clock – each head contains hundreds of seeds, each with its individual parachute, and each was originally one flower.

In members of asteraceae, which look like the typical 'daisy', there are two sorts of florets: ray florets, which comprise the outer ring of often brightly coloured 'petals', and disc florets that form the centre of the flowerhead. To confuse matters further some have only disc florets – the burdock, or 'sticky bobs' as we used to call them, have only disc florets whereas the dandelion and its ilk have only ray florets.

The fields around our house are full of dandelions, and when they are in seed our dogs, Fifi and Fleur, look as though they've been having a pillow fight – they return from a romp in the field covered in white fluff. There are plants here and there all around my garden, impossible to remove in some cases where they have seeded between brick paths. We enjoy the first flowers, bright, new and a vital source of nectar and pollen for the first bees and early-flying butterflies. Before they set seed (theoretically), we pull them out. Their foliage is a great addition to the compost heap as their roots delve down so deeply they bring minerals up to the leaves.

We don't have a lawn anymore, but when we did – for a short time when our daughters were little – it was always referred to as 'the grass'. I encouraged speedwell and daisies to grow there just to make it less of a monoculture than

ABOVE
Dog daisies, moon daisies, ox-eye daisies – the essence of a summer's day.

OPPOSITE
The ubiquitous daisy of our lawns and fields is really worth a closer look.

it would otherwise have been. *Bellis perennis*, the daisy of lawns and cropped grasslands, is a delightful little plant and an important source of nectar and pollen for insects. This is the flower portrayed in children's drawings, a circle with petals attached around the edge. Is it the most familiar flower? City dwellers and those who live in the countryside all recognise it, know it and feel an affinity with it. As children, and adults too given half a chance, we make daisy-chains with it. We search for jam-daisies with deep pink on the reverse of their petals and marvel at the way each flower closes its petals at the day's end and opens them wide in the morning. It is the eye of the day – the day's eye.

Dandelions, thistles and dog daisies are amongst our most common indigenous daisies. Each one sets the season, reminding us of where the year has reached. Once upon a time dog daisies, moon daisies and ox-eye daisies were a common sight but numbers have dwindled. During the last few years dog daisies carpeting road verges has, thankfully, become an increasingly common sight. The fact that they have also asserted their presence on motorway embankments is good reason for a hearty round of applause.

This relaxed, informal plant, with its simple big white daisies lit with a golden disc, makes people feel happy. It is summer personified. Usually at its best in June and July, sometimes it puts on an even longer display. Both last year and this it got into its stride early, and by mid-April the emerging grasses were lit by its white 'moons'. Often it keeps going strong late into the autumn – a non-stop show of dazzling proportions. It can cope with torrential rain and floods because of its creeping, mat-forming habit – its roots spread themselves out widely but are just below the surface of the soil, creating broad mats composed of dense foliage. By the same token it seems to manage almost as well in periods of prolonged drought, mulching the ground with its own basal foliage.

If it is so successful, why don't we see more of it? The answer, as with so many of our dwindling wild flowers, is simple. It is because they have been sprayed with herbicides, rooted out and scythed to the ground. They have always tended to stick to the field edges and hedgerows rather than insinuate themselves amongst crops. Because they are perennials they would not survive the rigours of being ploughed each year, unlike their close relative the corn marigold, which relies upon the annual tillage of the soil to distribute its seeds. Cornfield weeds, as farmers call them, are all annuals.

Perhaps the dog daisy is too invasive to be introduced into polite society, but there is no reason why it should not be grown in a big pot in the garden. Use soil-based compost and line your pot with a plastic bag, or an old compost bag, punctured for drainage. Plants can be bought as plugs or started from seed. One seedhead saved from a plant will yield scores of seed, and if it is sprinkled on the surface of a half-tray or large pot filled with seed compost, germination will be rapid and seedlings easy to grow on. When we made a garden, 21 Century Street, at the RHS Chelsea Flower Show, we wanted to illustrate how simple it was for anyone to introduce wild flowers into their own plot. We built a tiny wild-flower garden, but also introduced wild flowers into the main garden in the form of 'wild-flower pots'. They all contained a collection of indigenous flowers and grasses, including dog daisies, all grown from seed.

Cultivated cousins

Daisies are a huge and important group of plants. For those who prefer to stick to 'cultivated' daisies (although this may be a contradiction in terms since the great majority we use in our gardens are wild flowers from some other part of the world), there are plenty to choose from.

For our purposes, those we are most interested in are daisies from temperate regions akin to our own. Of course there are a few exceptions, such as the little Mexican daisy, *Erigeron karvinskianus*, that has established itself not only in the South West, but increasingly on walls much further north. It is a charming plant whose white daisies become deep pink as they age and, though it will seed itself into every nook and cranny it can find, it could never become a nuisance. Another 'Mexican' daisy, the

dahlia, has been living happily here for at least two hundred years.

There are zinnias, calendulas, catananche, echinops, eupatorium, gallardia, inula, tagetes and osteospermum – the list really is endless.

Many of our best daisies originate further north in the Americas, in the USA and Canada. Many were prairie plants, although their natural habitat has disappeared with the same dismaying rapidity as our meadows, home of our moon daisies. The Michaelmas daisies belong to this group – *Aster novae-angliae* (from New England) and *Aster novi-belgii* (New York was called New Belgium) are good examples.

So many of our mainstay border daisies come from North America, including heleniums with their bronze and yellow door-knob centres surrounded by floppy petals in rich rusts, oranges and yellows. Also helianthus, perennial sunflowers – many of which reach 1.8m (6ft) high – and rudbeckias, often called Black-eyed Susan. Almost without exception these are robust daisies, used to the hurly-burly of life on the prairie, of competing with grasses in a scrubby setting, and are therefore ideal to use in a similar context as a crucial part of our beds and borders.

OPPOSITE TOP LEFT
Bellis perennis, 'the day's eye', every child's first favourite flower.
TOP RIGHT
From Mexico, *Erigeron karvinskianus* has become a common sight.

OPPOSITE BELOW
Clouds of soft blue from *Aster* 'Little Carlow', here with fellow daisies *Helianthus* 'Lemon Queen' and *Rudbeckia fulgida* var. *deamii*.

At the end of the summer, and as autumn sets in, waves of rudbeckia and asters eclipse all earlier excitements in the garden at Glebe Cottage. The pinks, purples and magenta of July's geraniums are overtaken. Clouds of early Michaelmas daisies provide complementary contrasts to the all-pervading glow from golds, yellows, oranges and reds, and take the daisy's reign through into the last part of the year.

Michaelmas daisies epitomise autumn. See them and you can almost hear the crunch of crisp, fallen leaves underfoot and smell the bonfire smoke. They are born survivors. Chunks discarded from gardens set up home on railway embankments or decorate road verges with clouds of white or hazy blue. These are cultivars only once removed from their wild predecessors, plants of the American prairies superseded nowadays by a race of multi-coloured hybrids.

In the top part of our long, sloping garden, in an area with small beds and a series of brick paths, there are two brick platforms with seats where visitors can sit and enjoy the garden. Poking through the slats of one of them are voluminous clouds of blue. These daisies look particularly lovely on dull days, early mornings or in the late afternoon. When the sun shines, flotillas of autumn-hatched butterflies – red admirals, peacocks and tortoiseshells – make a beeline for them to feast on their rich nectar. This is *Aster cordifolius* 'Little Carlow', always trouble-free and reliable. Its flowers are so tightly packed they almost look like one enormous flower. Even though it is growing amongst the roots of a cherry tree, its foliage has remained pristine – not a trace of mildew. It's commonly known as the wood aster, as its wild relatives grow on the outskirts of woodland and its ability to cope with shade make it a very versatile plant – some daisies can even cope with shady sites. There are daisies for everywhere and everyone.

OPPOSITE
Autumn-flowering daisies are the first pit-stop for newly hatched butterflies.
ADOVE
Admiral on *Aster* 'Little Carlow'.
BELOW LEFT
And on *Rudbeckia hirta* 'Rustic Dwarfs'.
BELOW RIGHT
Speckled wood enjoying *Rudbeckia fulgida* var. *deamii*.

LATE SUMMER INTO AUTUMN

As summer progresses, the mood changes. Celebrations continue but now it's an all-night party. There is no let-up, and as the garden burgeons, the volume is turned up. There are peaks and more peaks, the crest of the wave runs and runs. Everywhere plants are ebullient, flowering themselves to the very edge of their existence, giving their all.

But some days are quiet. There are dog days, when the hot air turns everything ashimmer, waves of heat distort the horizon and the fields seems to undulate. The only discernible sound is the background hum of insects. After disappointing summers it's difficult to remember that sometimes it's so hot during July and August that you can't put your bare feet down on stone or slate, and have to dance your way to the nearest shade.

Borders are groaning with the weight of flowers, drenched in colour. So many plants are at the height of their performance now.

Giant bellflowers erupt into heads of blue flower, bringing a glow to summer evenings. They mingle with achilleas and the multifarious heads of jet-black or palest-lemon scabious. This is the season for neighbourliness, plants stand cheek by jowl, reaching the zenith of their growth.

There is a competitive element too, both in the civilized environs of the garden and out in the hurly-burly of the hedgerow. Along lanes and roadsides, even in unlikely venues, on traffic roundabouts and waste lots, plants are reaching their crescendo. The intriguing platforms of wild carrot brush with the strong stems of knapweed, hard heads, in a race to impress and bring in the bees. At the seaside, sand dunes sparkle with glaucous marram grass and silvery sea hollies.

Then, before you know it, the hullabaloo begins to subside. Vivid colour starts to fade. The vibrancy of high summer is replaced by the subtle onset of autumn. Some of us find it difficult to enjoy gardens at this time of year. There is nothing fresh and zingy. But spring is the time for all that razzmatazz.

Colour now is mellow and warm. It seeps into the consciousness inexorably, russet and amber, crimson and bronze. All is quieting down. The retina-searing reds and vivid oranges and blues of high summer are gone. Grasses hold sway.

The palette may be narrower now, but it is much deeper and full of subtlety. And though all autumn colour is a sign of imminent expiration, that somehow makes it all the more poignant.

Legumes

Vetch, clover, sainfoin, gorse, broom and peas are some of our most familiar and widespread wild flowers. Individually each flower is small, though when they are clustered together into flowerheads they become much more visible. When those flowerheads are voluminous as when purple vetch cascades over hedges or flowering gorse smothers moorland, they are unmissable – and resplendent. All belong to the pea family, cultivated members of which form a hugely important part of our diet and as fodder for the animals we keep. At the same time all legumes help improve growing conditions, both for themselves and for their neighbours, through nodules on their roots that help make nitrogen available.

Vetch and clover used to be important plants in grassland, both for direct grazing and as a constituent of hay for winter feed. With the wholesale advent of Italian rye grass for sileage, such meadows were on the wane but thinking farmers, especially of the organic variety, are reintroducing clover.

Both red and white clover are important plants for bees. White clover is a long-lived perennial that spreads itself by stolons, making dense ground-covering clumps as do many other members of the pea family. *Lotus corniculatus*, known as bird's foot trefoil or eggs and bacon on account of the pinky-red tinge of its brilliant yellow flowers, grows in a similar way amongst grasses or on more open sites. Legumes are accommodating plants, though most have a predilection for sunshine with a few exceptions like the wood vetch.

Gorse, *Ulex europaeus*, is a real sun-lover and has been a vital plant to some communities. Not only was it gathered for fuel, but it was used for bedding, both for animals and humans, and as fodder – especially for sheep and horses. Since it's so spiny you'd hope that in all these cases the prickly problem would have been addressed, and apparently there were gorse mills to crush and bruise the gorse prior to its being used as fodder. The sight of gorse, even on a dull day, is inspiring – great golden globs of scintillating chrome-yellow, and when you get up close the unexpected treat of one of the most delicious perfumes ever, not just coconut but with extra sweetness - more like coconut ice cream.

Cultivated cousins

In our gardens legumes are indispensable, not just on the vegetable plot in the form of beans and peas but in the ornamental garden. Lupins are the obvious example – cottage-garden favourites, they have come a long way since their introduction from America in the early 19th century. Most make bold spires of colour early in the herbaceous border's display. The great majority of lupin fanciers, in my limited experience, are men. Could it be that many male

OPPOSITE
Vetch is important for insects, for livestock and for the health of the soil.

gardeners (but not all, I hasten to add) admire the uniformity of their upright stems? Tree lupins are more to my taste, usually pale, washed-out yellow with scores, sometimes hundreds, of flower spikes and an engaging scent.

Trifolium ochroleucum is a most lovely clover of a similar colour. In the fertile soil at Glebe Cottage it reaches half a metre and spreads as much across. In an open bed in full sun, and with excellent drainage, it is more compact and needs no staking. Its large heads of small flowers are wonderfully rotund and their pale-lemon colour is almost impossible to mismatch. It goes with just about everything with the possible

OPPOSITE TOP LEFT
The pretty spring sweet pea, *Lathyrus vernus,* here *L. v.* 'Alboroseus'.
TOP RIGHT
Hedysarum coronarium, a spectacular pea used as a fodder crop around the Mediterranean but a star of the show in the border.
BELOW LEFT
Crimson-flowered broad bean – we use this ornamentally too.
BELOW RIGHT
A delightful clover, *Trifolium ochroleucum,* making scores of flowers in a season.

exception of bright yellow, which kills it and makes it look washed-out. It is perhaps at its best alongside pastels where it brings a citric edge that seems to sharpen up the mixture. Striking too with dark foliage, try it alongside one of the bronze-leaved forms of *Geranium pratense*.

In common with other legumes, broad beans make handsome plants and look just as much at home in the midst of a flower border as they do in serried ranks in the veg plot. They are strong plants, eager to grow, with attractive foliage, often glaucous, borne in whorls around the stems. The dense clusters of flowers, white with a chocolate splodge, are sweetly perfumed to attract pollinators. A few heritage varieties have deep-pink flowers. As they fade the tiny pods begin to grow, eventually swelling to fat, waxy pods, shiny, robust and very, very green. Podding broad beans is a sensual delight. The hard, shiny casing could not be more different from the furry interiors where the young beans nestle so comfortably. They should be picked successively, just before they reach maturity when the pod is tight with its cargo, but before it reaches bursting point. Broad beans need to be eaten young and fresh.

With a salad of young broad beans on the table, a jug of sweet peas nearby and the garden full of lupins, baptisia and hedysarum, not to mention robinia, laburnums and brooms, we gardeners have much to thank the pea family for. And all this is nothing in comparison to the usefulness of them and their wild cousins to our pollinating insects.

Bellflowers

We are lucky enough to have several campanulas, or bellflowers, amongst our native wild flowers. Perhaps the harebell is the most widely known and most dearly cherished of them all. It is a whisper of a flower, hardly there yet enormously tenacious. From tiny rosettes of neat, rounded leaves fine stems push up bearing dainty pleated buds that are at first erect, but later hang down as the bells start to open to protect the pollen secreted within from gale and tempest. Widespread throughout the British Isles, it is a flower of open, exposed venues – of moor and mountainside, of cliff-top. We filmed it near Bridlington, glittering amongst fine, dense grass. My mum and I saw it, running in ribbons across the limestone pavement of The Burren, growing in next to nothing. We met it on another occasion too in the Yorkshire Dales, on a sunny day growing in springy turf. We had no choice than to abandon socks and shoes and enjoy the feel of the grass between our toes, surrounded by these happy flowers.

Campanula rotundifolia needs little nutrient and often the poorer its soil, the more profusely will it flower. When we filmed our little campanula film, having seen harebells on the cliff-top, we went to Burton Agnes Hall, where atop the big, old, curved brick walls which guide you in under an imposing arch to the drive up to the magnificent house, harebells have made themselves at home-seeding generously in the lime mortar between the coping stones. Blue against blue with an azure sky above.

Cultivated cousins

Surely bellflowers are one of the most enchanting of all plant families. Most herbaceous campanulas have soft leaves (*C. latifolia*, *C. lactiflora* and *C. glomerata* are examples), whereas evergreen campanulas, *C. persicifolia* and *C. latiloba* and many of the lobelias, have harder, shinier foliage. Bellflowers are versatile, gracious and easy to grow.

Their blue flowers create restful spaces in a sea of busy colour, lending distance and depth to plantings teetering on the brink of confusion. Those that make the boldest impact are big

OPPOSITE
Campanula rotundifolia, the harebell, wiry and tough, yet wistful and poetic.
ABOVE
Campanula latifolia, another of our native bellflowers. This is a selection called 'Gloaming'.

campanulas, some of them up to 1.5–1.8m (5–6ft) tall. Some have symmetry, others rely on a wafty loftiness to command the scene.

Many of these resplendent flowers would have featured in the traditional herbaceous border; Miss Jekyll writes of them with affection and included them in many of her planting schemes. But there is nothing old-hat about them – their uses are legion. They can be employed as individual container plants, repeated on a terrace or down steps or, for maximum impact, in naturalistic planting schemes. One plant could make the centre of a special cameo, or bold clumps could be repeated along a border to give a feeling of integrity.

For the most part they are blue often verging on purple, lilac or misty grey. Some are white. All of them are best viewed as the sun sets or comes up, or in shade or on a cloudy day, when their colour is most telling.

Top of the list is *Campanula lactiflora* – aptly named the milky bellflower, it is one of the most appealing of all bellflowers. When it is blue there is white mixed in, when it is white its flowers are tinged with blue creating the 'milky' impression. This is emphasised when it is seen in shade, where it grows just as happily as it does in full sun. On good ground it can make 1.5m (5ft) easily, its large heads of small, clustered bells gracefully overlooking lesser plants. If you prefer more definite colour there is a deep–blue selection, *C. lactiflora* 'Prichard's Variety'. While you can raise a nice mixture from seed, 'Prichard's Variety' must be propagated vegetatively, either from division or by taking short, basal cuttings in the spring. Stems must be solid, as once they are hollow this method doesn't work.

One of the bellflowers that was once used extensively in pots, *C. pyramidalis*, is essentially a biennial and must be raised from seed year on year. Its vernacular name, the chimney bellflower, is apt as it makes a central stem from a rosette of basal leaves, which can reach he-man size, 1.8m (6ft), clustered round with separate bells. Its upright bearing makes it a perfect plant for a formal entrance where it can act as a sentry.

In the days when nursery labour was cheap, *Ostrowskia magnifica* could be found on many a nurseryman's list. It was propagated then from basal cuttings – a practice no longer considered commercially viable today. 'Magnifica' is no exaggeration – huge substantial bells, white with a hint of grey and a darker centre, hang individually from tall elegant stems. It needs deep fertile soil and the protection of a warm wall.

OPPOSITE TOP LEFT
Campanula trachelium 'Bernice'. A fancy double-flowered form of our native nettle-leaved bellflower.
TOP RIGHT
Campanula alliariifolia 'Ivory Bells'.
BELOW LEFT
There are a plethora of double-flowered forms of *Campanula persicifolia*. This bonny beauty is *C. p.* 'Wortham Belle'.
BELOW RIGHT
Campanula glomerata 'Superba' can be forgiven its slightly thuggish habits because of its all-round dependability.

Some campanulas make an impact not from their height, but from the weight and volume of their bells and, in some cases, their colour. C. 'Sarastro' bears large, purple-blue waxy bells opening from folded, slender buds of deepest purple. It is a recent cultivar and probably the progeny of a cross between our own *C. latifolia* and one of the long-belled asiatic bellflowers, *C. takesimana* or *C. punctata*. A sterile hybrid, it flowers all summer long. Cut the flowering stems to ground level when they are finished, and more will be forthcoming within a few weeks. Should you prefer deep-blue to purple *C.* 'Kent Belle', with a similar parentage, is the one to go for.

Some of our native bellflowers are as beautiful and useful in the garden as any. *C. latifolia*, the nettle-leaved bellflower, is most commonly blue or white, but there is a variety with subtle pale-lilac flowers which is particularly prevalent along the riverbanks of north-east England and Scotland. A cultivar, *C. latifolia* 'Gloaming', boasts flowers of the same hue and has the added attraction of dark-purple centres, which can also be seen on the outside of the bell. It gradually builds year by year to form a statuesque clump up to 90cm (3ft) in height and 60cm (2ft) across.

Grey is a colour seldom seen in flowers, and while it may sound unattractive, it is often a glorious addition to a humdrum scheme, bringing a touch of class to the proceedings. *C.* 'Burghaltii' has pale, grey-lilac flowers. No one is quite sure of its origins, but everyone agrees it is graceful and elegant. Despite its subtle

demeanour, it is always noticed. Anyone would welcome it into their garden.

Summer borders are places where plants need to get on well, no room for prima donnas here, and bellflowers are great team players. One of the most persistent in my garden is *C. persicifolia*. It is one of the most beautiful and poetic of summer garden flowers. It forms evergreen rosettes of narrow, pointed leaves giving it its common name, the peach-leaved bellflower. From midsummer onwards, straight stems shoot up vertically from the low, carpeting foliage until, at about 60cm (2ft), they stop to concentrate on opening their fat buds. The species plant has simple, single bells in blue or white. It seeds prolifically and seedlings may vary in flower colour and stature, and occasionally in form. If double forms are to your liking, there are all sorts to choose from, some frilly, others cup and saucer and, my favourite, which is a blue cup-in-cup with one flower held within another. We make more in early spring by dividing up the rosettes – we can't have too many!

In classic bellflowers each bell has five points or tips, and each seed capsule is divided into three chambers. Campanulaceae distribute

OPPOSITE
There is a huge range of alpine bellflowers ideal for walls, troughs and rock gardens.
TOP LEFT
Campanula 'Royal Wave'.

TOP RIGHT
Campanula portenschlagiana makes itself at home.
OPPOSITE BELOW
A tiny beauty, *Campanula cochleariifolia* 'Elizabeth Oliver'.

their seed in an unusual way: small apertures appear at the back of the capsule as it begins to brown and dry, and eventually seed is scattered through these holes. It was while waiting to collect seed from an especially lovely *C. latifolia* that I realised this, but by the time what was happening dawned on me, it had all gone. Campanula seed is very fine and there's lots of it, but be sure to move in with paper bags and scissors before it disperses. On the whole growing campanulas from seed is a straightforward, exciting and cheap way to build up your stock.

If big bellflowers are to live happily and develop their true character, they need sustenance. Although the great majority are happy on alkaline soils, gardeners with thin, chalky soils or light sandy soils need to give them preferential treatment, so amend the conditions to give them as rich a diet as possible. Adding bulky organic matter helps, and frequent feeding should be part of the regime.

June and July are their months, although the season can be extended by cutting back flowered stems and feeding plants with a liquid feed – we use an organic seaweed extract.

Sea hollies

Just a few miles from where we live are several beaches renowned for their sand and surf. Along from one of them, Saunton Sands, is a nature reserve, Braunton Burrows, that boasts many wonderful maritime plants. For me the jewel in its crown is *Eryngium maritimum* – the true sea holly. There are two miles of sand dunes and if you are lucky enough to be there in July you will discover amongst the sand and marram grass, patches of ghostly silvery blue. As you get closer across the dunes, the plants become more and more distinct until you are close enough to appreciate in detail what must be one of the most charismatic of all our wild flowers.

At summer's peak, rounded clumps of herbaceous perennials are very satisfying in a border – rather like a Beryl Cook painting, a room full of plump women all dolled up for a party. But their curvaceous image is made all the more reassuring by a contrast or two. A few spiky characters can provide just what is needed, and none does it more effectively

than eryngium. Sea hollies are a spiny, prickly bunch. In the case of the European species both leaves and the bracts (or cyathium leaves), which surround their flowers, are well-armed to protect flowers and precious seed from marauding animals intent on grazing everything in sight.

Eryngium belong to the genus apiaceae. Until a short time ago they were classified as umbelliferae. It's hard to see at first what they have in common with the frothy platforms of cow parsley, the kind of plant that usually springs to mind when umbels are mentioned. Archetypal umbels bear their tiny flowers, usually in great numbers, in flat heads, whereas in sea hollies the flowers are clustered together around a raised central cone.

There are two groups of sea hollies – one from Europe and Eurasia and one from Central and South America – whose characteristics are very different. The Old World species have rosettes of low foliage, sometimes rounded or waved and often patterned or marbled in white. Their flowers are surrounded by bracts, small in

OPPOSITE AND ABOVE
To find our native sea holly luxuriating in the sun on its home ground – or home sand – was one of the most uplifting moments of our day at the seaside.

some of the more branching species, but large and very decorative in those with fewer, stronger stems and flowers.

Those from the New World have enormous basal rosettes composed of immensely long green leaves, barbed at their edges. The impression is that of a holly leaf, which has been stretched to a ridiculous length – some of them can be more than 1.8m (6ft) long. Their flowers too are superficially different to those of most of their European cousins. They are small and bobbly, in hosts along the tall, branching stems, or clamped around the top of thick stems in species such as *E. agavifolium*. They have green flowers occasionally touched by crimson. Most are plants of damp, open ground, their huge stems often zooming up through long grass, towering over the pampas. Many are too big for all but the very largest gardens, and their immense spiny leaves make them even more anti-social. Some of the smaller species (which are still substantial) are good garden plants where something monumental is called for, providing strong structure for a long period.

Cultivated cousins

E. agavifolium is easier to accomodate than most, reaching a modest 1.8m (6ft) by 60cm (2ft) wide. As its name denotes, its broad, fleshy leaves are set with spines. It prefers drier ground than most in its group but nonetheless needs adequate moisture in the summer. It has great presence and makes an ideal focal point. If the ground is damper then *E. eburneum* might make a suitable alternative. It is much the same size, with more branching flowerheads of greeny-white and much narrower leaves.

If you have enough space *E. horridum*, with narrow grass-like leaves, has widely branching flower stems covered with small, pale bobbles. It is spectacular. *E. pandanifolium* bears multitudes of tiny crimson flowers on towering stems.

From Mexico, *E. proteiflorum* is strikingly different with large bracts of silvery white. Once you see it you feel you must have it, though few of us could keep it very long. Perfect drainage and a very sheltered position in a warm garden would give it the best chance

One of the most endearing characteristics of sea hollies is the longevity of their display. Most have evergreen leaves and the flowers of both groups last for a long time, continuing to look good when they have turned to seed. The more showy species amongst the European group have the bonus of bracts which often keep their form and colour for months. Their flowerheads often persist deep into the coldest months, their colour fading to buffs and browns in keeping with the winter scene.

E. bourgatii, from the mountains of Europe, is exceptional. The midribs and veins of its spiky basal foliage are picked out in silvery white giving it a shimmery effect and making attractive basal foliage even in midwinter. In the best forms the silvery green flowers with their large bracts turn gradually to the deepest blue. Reaching only 45cm (18in), this is an ideal plant for small gardens. It combines perfectly with pale yellow *Achillea* Anthea or the lemon daisies of *Anthemis* 'E. C. Buxton'. There are named forms of *Eryngium bourgatii*, but any plant whose flowers turn brilliant blue will yield seed that will itself produce blue-flowered progeny and sometimes the children may be better than their parents. At Glebe Cottage we always try to mark the best plants for seed collection, occasionally with a note on the label recording any special characteristics such as 'the best blue with very big flowers with narrow bracts'. Probably the most charismatic of all the sea-hollies, *E. alpinum* has a lacy ruff around its flowers. They are rich, true blue and although the plant gives the impression of being heavily armed it is in fact soft to the touch.

Although the genus is renowned for its perennial contingent there are biennials too, one of which is especially valued for its ornamental qualities. *E. giganteum* is often known as Miss Wilmott's ghost. The story goes that Ellen Wilmott would scatter the seed here and there in gardens she was visiting wherever she felt that they needed a bit of invigoration. Once you have it, it will haunt your garden forever.

Sea hollies are an easy-going bunch providing they have the conditions they need. The South American species like damp ground but do not like to paddle in the winter. Incorporate plenty of humus at planting time and provide a good mulch. European and Eurasian species and hybrids need sharp drainage but thrive best in good deep soil. They are self-supporting and should never need staking, although overfeeding, especially with high-nitrogen fertiliser or manure, will result in over-rapid growth and floppy stems. Grow species such as *E. planum* and *E.* × *tripartitum* as hard as possible. If you want to grow *E. maritimum*, our native coastal plant and the only true sea holly, raise it from seed and give it what it is used to – pure sand. All sea hollies love an open site in full sun, although dress acid soils with lime or calcified seaweed.

New World eryngiums can only be reproduced from seed, they are impossible to divide and root cuttings don't work. The European species are easy from seed but you can also make more with root cuttings – essential if you want to guarantee duplicates.

Scabious

Many of our wild flowers need searching out – they are quiet, retiring plants. In contrast there are a few that disport themselves gaily, showing any passerby just how special they are. From June through till October, and sometimes into November, the field scabious, *Knautia arvensis*, is just such a beauty, flaunting its pincushion heads of pale blue or lavender on road verges and field margins. It can take a foothold in practically any sunny place, but almost always on chalky or other alkaline soils. The field scabious is as beautiful in seed as it is in flower, and for months both seedheads and flowers combine to provide food for both butterflies and birds.

The small scabious, *Scabiosa columbaria*, enjoys similar conditions but is fairly tolerant. We have several thriving plants on the corner of our 'sea-side' patch. The only alkaline addition there to our neutral soil has been a few handfuls of old lime rubble when planting pinks close by. This pretty little plant is ideal for an alpine bed

– just as appropriate as is the field scabious for a meadow planting or a naturalistic border. On acid soil a third member of the group, devil's-bit scabious, *Succisa pratensis*, often crops up and seems to prefer damper conditions.

We grew our plants from seed. As with all scabious seed it is easy to gather, packed densely around a solid core. They look like mini-shuttlecocks and when they are ready to collect can be gently teased into your hand. Store in a paper bag or sow immediately on the surface of open compost and cover thinly with grit.

If scabious are attention seekers, there are some plants belonging to the same family, Dipsacaceae, that you just can't miss. Teasels are familiar to most of us, prominent plants standing individually as sentinels or more frequently in great hordes on road verges and wasteland, and increasingly ascending the slopes on motorway embankments.

Cultivated cousins

Wild scabious and teasels grow well in our gardens. So too do other members of the family. Several of them can be raised easily from seed, which is much more widely available than was the case just a few years ago, and once

ABOVE
Though teasels belong to the scabious clan, the resemblance isn't immediately obvious. They provide nectar for insects and seed for birds, and in summer their calyces operate as mini-reservoirs for thirsty birds.

OPPOSITE
Devil's-bit scabious, with a hundred or more tiny flowers for foraging bees to feed from.

you have your own plants you can continue to collect seed from them. A preference for more relaxed, naturalistic schemes has led to many scabious becoming increasingly popular. Most seem to enjoy mixing and mingling with other herbaceous plants and grasses.

Often described as an annual, the sweet scabious, *Scabiosa atropurpurea*, will often last two or three years. It makes a tall branching plant up to 1m (40in). Some of the colour forms are a bit wishy-washy, but very dark cultivars such as 'Chat Noir' or 'Ace of Spades' add rich and dramatic colour, especially when lit with white anthers. A newer plant for us is a big, beautiful, blue scabious, with the same habit of growth as *S. atropurpurea* but much bigger flowers. It was grown originally from seed from a plant at Berryfields, but there seem to be several on the market going under different names including one that calls itself 'Oxford Blue'. It is irresistible to both gardeners and butterflies.

Gardeners and insects alike adore the scabious family. The flowering strategies of the genus have evolved in symbiosis with the insects that pollinate them. From a gardener's point of view they satisfy so many criteria. You could be forgiven for thinking their decorative qualities had been created just for us. Initially it is their blatant flower-power that lures us in. Every member of the family produces an abundance of flowers, and most do so continuously from the long hot days of June through to the quiet muted wind-down of late autumn. Long and prolific flowering maximises any plant's chance of pollination, and therefore of seed production and distribution.

A good clump of *Knautia macedonica*, a much-prized European species, will contribute hundreds of its deep alizarin pincushions over one season.

It is the most asked-about plant in our garden. This is partly because it is so outstanding, but also because it is in flower longer than any other plant. Visitors' questions about 'those dark crimson pom-poms' roll in from May till November. From its vigour, it is evident that it is easy to grow, and from the striking beauty and number of its flowers it is clearly very desirable. Knautia, pronounced naughtier (which is another endearing feature), used to be called *Scabiosa rumelica*. It is clearly a member of the scabious family, Dipsacaceae, with a typical central dome of fertile florets, surrounded by a skirt of decorative petals which increase the flower's size and thereby its impact.

From a central rootstock it spreads out into a broad, chalice-shaped bush, each shoot branching and branching again until a broad wiry network of stems is formed. Every shoot and side-shoot terminates in a flower. Established plants produce literally hundreds in a season. Individual flowers last no longer than a fortnight but turn into spherical seedheads

OPPOSITE
We use *Scabiosa columbaria* subsp. *ochroleuca* in sunny spots in different parts of the garden. It is tolerant, easy and bears its delightful lemony pin-cushions for months. It's easy from seed and young plants can be potted individually and grown on.

of magical symmetry. In most cases gardening gurus advocate deadheading summer flowers to prolong quality flower production. In the case of *Knautia macedonica* this is both unnecessary and unwise. Not only do the seedheads enhance the plant (plants which have undergone deadheading surgery look peculiarly awry), but they are important food for birds. In common with all scabious, this is a highly useful wildlife plant, providing nectar for hoverflies, bees and butterflies. Because of the longevity of its flowering, autumn-hatched butterflies, which have more limited sources of food than early hatchings, can feast at the knautia bar until the end of the season.

Try it with other crimson flowers and foliage, close to pink or white roses to carry on the show. It will take over from flashy oriental poppies and early summer bulbs, alliums and camassia. Or encourage it to share the stage with *Scabiosa columbaria* subsp. *ochroleuca*, whose pale lemon bobbles emphasise the opulence of the knautias colouring as they dance together.

From the ground-hugging silver tufts of *S. graminifolia*, sprinkled with pinky mauve flowers, to the towering stems of the summer border colossus, *Cephalaria gigantea*, there are scabious for every site – as long as it is sunny and reasonably well-drained.

Scabiosa caucasica is the classic perennial scabious. Both its blue form, *S. caucasica* 'Clive Greaves', and the delightful white 'Miss Willmott' are cherished both as border stalwarts and cut flowers. Their enlarged marginal florets turn heads. Try as I might, they give up the ghost within months of being planted in my heavy cold clay. As well as better drainage, they would also doubtless prefer higher alkalinity than my neutral pH soil can offer.

So although I yearn for the poetry their ample elegant flowers offer, I opt for less fussy scabious. *S.* 'Butterfly Blue' and *S.* 'Pink Mist' go on with gay abandon, their rounded clumps getting bigger and better every year. Both seem to be fairly tough and long-lived. *Knautia arvensis*, our native field scabious, commonly occurs where conditions are on the alkaline side. Where it thrives it grows amongst soft grasses, deschampsia and Yorkshire fog, creating soft drifts with subtle nuances of colour – worth emulating and, for your version, you can choose grasses that will fit your site. In a garden setting, forms of *Scabiosa atropurpurea* can be used in the same way.

Always leave the seedheads of scabious. Not only do they add another dimension to the picture – all have a superb geodesic-dome structure – but they provide food for hungry birds and, with a bit of luck, masses of free self-sown seedlings.

OPPOSITE TOP LEFT
The whole scabious family make rewarding garden plants, from the aptly named *Cephalaria gigantea*, to the lower clump-forming plants.
TOP RIGHT
Knautia macedonica.

BELOW LEFT
Short-lived but long-flowering *Scabiosa atropurpurea.*
BELOW RIGHT
A classic Scabious, *S. caucasica* 'Perfecta Blue'.

Yarrow

Though they now seem to be a distant memory, in the past we have had summers that sizzled, where by the end of July grass in the fields around Glebe Cottage was dry and brown. Yet here and there amongst the all-pervading parchment were patches of green and white – it was yarrow, not only surviving but thriving. Even in years where the weather is typically wet, and drought is not a problem, the big splashes of chalky white that yarrow provides are always welcome – fresh and new at field edge and road verge, at a time of year when you can already feel that the inexorable slide towards autumn has already begun.

Achilleas are members of asteraceae, the erstwhile compositae clan. In other words, daisies. Each flat head of flower is composed of a score or more of tiny daisies, with their typical ray and disc florets. Instead of having fairly large and obvious daisies, like those of a rudbeckia or a dahlia, achillea flowers are tiny but there are lots more of them. They create an entirely different effect. Their stems seldom branch, except at the top where smaller stems divide off, each holding one tiny flower in much the same way as an umbel would support its flowers to form a plateau. The stems and the skinny, much divided leaves that run their length are hairy, both their texture and their skinniness denoting their ability to cope with dry conditions. At the foot of the stems the basal leaves spread out to form dense mats, keeping roots cool and retaining moisture.

Achilleas are stayers. At every stage of their flowers' development, even when dying, they make an outstanding contribution to the summer show. In recent years, using cultivars of *Achillea millefolium* has become the thing in naturalistic and prairie plantings. They are immensely useful wenders and weavers, insinuating themselves amongst other clumpier plants. Each flat head is composed of scores of tiny flowers clustered together to form plateaux held on stiff stems. The centre of each tiny daisy is paler than the surrounding petals, giving the flowerhead the look of something from a pointillist painting. Excitingly the flower colour changes from week to week.

OPPOSITE AND ABOVE
Yarrow, *Achillea millefolium*, is a survivor, keeping its freshness and sparkle even in drought. Each head is composed of scores of tiny daisies.

Cultivated cousins

In a blue and yellow summer scheme in a sunny situation, the heads of lemon achilleas are perfect. Particularly attractive are several varieties with grey, woolly foliage. Reaching knee height, *A.* 'Moonshine', hybridised and introduced by Alan Bloom, is an excellent plant that needs no staking or fuss. As with all achilleas, though the flower colour eventually fades, the flowerheads maintain their structure. If something taller is needed, *A.* 'Credo' has 90cm (3ft) stems topped by pale-lemon heads. These yarrows are real July flowers, turning up the heat and instilling searing colour into the border. In recent years, Dutch, British and German hybridists have introduced a host of new cultivars, many with orange and red colouring, often verging on earthy brown. The cultivar 'Terracotta' has beautiful blooms that open clay-orange and fade to buff with age.

'Marmalade', 'McVities' and 'Walther Funcke' are all exciting, as are any of the Forncett Series developed by John Metcalf, one of the foremost plant breeders around, who has a real eye for a good plant.

Achilleas answer the demand for informal plants, good mixers, to mingle and fraternise with other border belles. They are traditional border flowers, valued for their feathery foliage and for their striking, flat, circular heads of flowers throughout the main summer season. They team well with other perennial flowers, and are a vital ingredient of a traditional herbaceous border. They are also at home in island beds, cottage gardens and other perennial planting schemes, including wave planting!

Gardens are shrinking, but at the same time our horticultural ambitions are growing. Most of us are no longer content with a neat lawn surrounded by narrow borders and, as far as plants go, our sights are set higher than ever. We are more involved with our gardening too, and we expect our plots to do more for us. Many of us prefer a more naturalistic approach to the formal bedding of yesteryear, or the sometimes contrived heather'n'conifer combos of the 70s and 80s.

What about prairie planting? In private gardens with ample room, or in large municipal areas, prairie planting can be an ideal ethos. It is meant for the grand scale, a self-sustaining system where communities of plants naturalise and self-seed. On a small scale with tight boundaries and defined space it doesn't work – but wave planting does, and achilleas are one of its most suitable ingredients!

What is wave planting? It is a method (a very loose and unfettered one) of putting herbaceous plants and grasses together to create a dynamic picture. It incorporates a limited number of plant varieties, combined together so that each benefits aesthetically from its association with

OPPOSITE TOP LEFT
Daisies on different scales, *Achillea* 'Moonshine' and *Anthemis tinctoria* 'Sauce Hollandaise'.

TOP RIGHT AND BELOW
Achillea filipendulina 'Gold Plate' is a tried-and-tested yarrow, used in traditional borders and more adventurous schemes for decades.

its neighbours. Plants are arranged in waves across the border (not a straight line in sight), their heights vary and there is both contrast and close harmony within the planting.

In a typical border, narrower than it is long, arranging plants in a series of undulating waves from front to back can establish a rhythm, which constantly supplies movement from spring to winter. There are no arbitrary drifts arranged like interlocking crazy paving. Instead ribbons of plants sweep backwards and forwards so that wave upon wave laps against the next in continuous succession. There are no focal points or full stops. The whole planting flows.

The great boon of wave planting is that it is applicable to even a small bed, and to areas which are immutably rectangular – a typical scenario in a modern garden. All you need is a sense of adventure and a whole lot of plants. But because such schemes have straightforward plants at their heart, it is possible to create such a design with the minimum of expense if you are prepared to increase your own plants and have the patience to wait for them to grow. To me this is part of the journey and a huge lot of fun. On the way you also get to know your plants intimately.

By using plants whose persona changes during the season, and by choosing subjects with interesting foliage, flower and, where possible, seedheads, the scheme can provide ongoing interest and drama. Bulbs too can be incorporated to supply high points and extra panache. Success depends on choosing the right plants for your soil and situation (achilleas fit the bill perfectly), not stinting on numbers and focusing on sticking to the waves.

When achilleas are given lush growing conditions, they burgeon, making large flat heads on strong stems, but sometimes their very vigour can be their downfall. If a summer of over-exuberant growth is followed by a wet cold winter, they may succumb. Best to treat them badly, or at least ignore them.

There is no doubt that there are some plants that thrive on neglect, and achillea is a good example – it should never be overfed or have any great attention lavished upon it. If this seems cruel, it is really much more unfeeling to force-feed such a plant with applications of muck and fertilizer, when in fact its antecedents thrive on thin, poor, dry soils.

Given the sort of conditions they like, full sun and excellent drainage, they will go on happily for years. If clumps become congested, they can be easily pulled apart (spring is best) their old woody centres discarded and the new pieces planted in ordinary garden soil – without fuss and definitely without rich food!

OPPOSITE
Here with sea hollies and alliums, a softly coloured achillea is at its happiest and most relaxed.

Thistles

The thistle is the national emblem of Scotland – brave, proud and a bit prickly. There are a host of varieties, from the tall elegant spires of the aptly named melancholy thistle, with its slightly hanging buds and seedheads that give it a somewhat sad, dolorous air, to the defiant chunky spear thistle, upright and armed to the teeth defying any creature to take a munch. All thistles, though, welcome the attentions of pollinating insects and many employ scent as a lure. The beautiful and abundant creeping thistle that gardeners dread has some of the most fragrant flowers imaginable, with a rich, honeyed perfume, completely at odds with its viciously aggressive foliage.

Thistles grow in all kinds of places. They have evolved to cope with sites from bogs and marshes to parched wasteland. Leaves, roots, flowers and seedheads all play their part in the success story. Instead of petals or the ray florets of most asteraceae, their flowerheads consist of scores of closely packed disc florets with fine filaments giving the flowers their characteristic fluffy plateaux. They open in succession, often over a period of months, thus multiplying their chances of successful pollination. Most set copious seed and the 'parachute' method they employ for the distribution of the seed they set, accompanied by the attraction of those seeds to birds, guarantees their progress. Closely allied are the centaureas or knapweeds. When you see their purple powder puffs bursting from their hard, bronze calyces, you have no option than to recognize that the second half of summer is upon us.

Cultivated cousins

Once upon a time to include thistles in a garden setting was unthinkable. Nowadays they are invited, even welcomed into the very best gardens. In every venue from naturalistic plantings to the most proper herbaceous borders, thistles have become must-have. Farming myth has it that if a piece of ground supports thistles, it is liable to be fertile. Most thistles thrive on good soil, and though there are a few that can rough it on drier, thinner soil, the majority repay good cultivation and a rich living.

ABOVE
Tremendously successful, the creeping thistle spreads by roots and by seed launched on a million parachutes.

OPPOSITE
The marsh thistle, *Cirsium palustre*, is a much gentler individual. Its spines look alarming but are quite soft. Still, I wouldn't want to eat it!

Most are true perennials gracing the garden each summer and improving in stature year by year. A few, such as *Galactites tomentosa* and *Silybum marianum*, are biennial, making glorious rosettes in their first year and flowering themselves to oblivion in their second. Many have bold leaves and could be welcomed for their foliage alone. They provide a profusion of purple- or crimson-tufted blooms, and in some instances crunchy calyces and silken, fluffy seedheads.

Galactites tomentosa is a weed around the Mediterranean and in Iberia. In my garden it is greeted with delight any time it deigns to turn up. Self-sown seedlings lie flat against the soil like so many silvery starfish. Each rosette grows rapidly outwards until suddenly the flower stem erupts from the centre. Within a few weeks they are transformed into branching, bushy plants, their green stems iced with silver. Soon they will be adorned with tiny lilac thistles. They need nothing more than to be left to their own devices.

From Morocco's Atlas Mountains, *Ptilostemon afer* is one of the most striking of the genus. Wickedly barbed leaves (no self-respecting goat would ever dream of putting it on the menu), marbled in white, form-striking, basal rosettes. Their geometry is breathtaking

and once you have seen the plant there is no option but to grow it. Its flowering is both its zenith and its demise. Glorious big thistles are borne on 45cm (18in) stems. Once seed is set and distributed the plant dies. Save your own seed.

Thistles (and knapweeds) stand out from the run-of-the-mill clumps of more usual perennials, differentiating themselves from the crowd yet never looking at odds with their companions. Their flowering period starts in late May and extends through the summer into autumn. Once flowering is finished, many can be cut down to the ground, thus stimulating the production of new flowers, but where masses of seed is produced, we leave them – thistle seed is a great attraction to broad-billed birds, goldfinches and their ilk. In fact thistles are a useful addition to the garden for anyone interested in enticing wildlife. Without exception they are insect attractants, and nectar-sucking butterflies, bees, moths and hoverflies will all come to feast on their abundant flowers.

Cirsium rivulare 'Atropurpureum' has been much used over the past few years. With neatly trimmed flowers in rich crimson on tall stems, it makes a focal point from April through to July and August. It is worth chopping it down to the ground after its first flowering. In the early spring each plant makes a large basal rosette, or in older plants a collection of rosettes, each with embryonic buds at their core. As the leaves begin to assume a thistly look the stems soar upwards, reaching 1.2m (4ft) when growing in substantial soil.

OPPOSITE
Knapweeds are thistles without the armaments.
TOP LEFT
Centaurea glastifolia. Unusual but brilliant.
TOP RIGHT
Knapweed, hardheads, is a tough, robust plant, successfully colonising field edges and road verges.
OPPOSITE BELOW
Centaurea montana, a cottage garden favourite, easy and dependable.

Rivulare means growing by a stream, and this cirsium certainly seems to prefer damp and fertile ground. Some thistles are as exciting when in seed as they are in full flower. Not this one. Its soft seedheads look dishevelled especially after heavy rain and tend to break up. There's no seed either so cut them down to the ground when they've finished.

At a princely 1.8m (6ft), with large white spheres held on strong white stems, *Echinops bannaticus* 'Albus' makes a stately presence. More compact but still of goodly size – up to 1.2m (4ft) – the globe thistle, *Echinops ritro* subsp. *ruthenicus*, is a border stalwart – as its regular appearance in herbaceous borders far and wide attests. It has been in cultivation in our gardens for almost two centuries, and individual plants have a long life span, reliably producing their blue drumstick flowers throughout the summer. Even before the slender, individual flowers open, the spherical heads make an impact, silvery at first and gradually changing to blue as circle after circle of flowers opens. These are nectar rich but their long corolla tubes make the feast most easily available to moths with their elongated proboscis.

Like artichokes and cardoons, echinops can be increased by detaching side shoots with a sharp knife at their base in April and planting in situ with sand added to the planting hole. Water well until they are established. Plants will benefit from a mulch of good compost or old manure after being cut back. Delay this as long as possible since thistle seeds are a delicacy to finches. Butterflies, bees and hoverflies will visit thistle flowers constantly as they provide a rich source of nectar.

Although it is often called 'the Scotch thistle', *Onopordon acanthium* is a European plant and probably only native to parts of East Anglia. Its other vernacular title is cotton thistle, a very apt description of the soft fluffy surface of its leaves. This is a plant with two minds; despite this soft covering of both leaves and buds, a protection against hot sun, it is also armed to the teeth. Both the leaf rims and the buds are equipped with dangerous spines. Nonetheless if you want impact it is hard to beat. Grow it from seed and plant plenty for dramatic effect.

Perhaps knapweeds are not strictly thistles, but both belong to the genus asteracea, and while centaurea lack the armoury that most thistles possess, the construction of their flowers is identical. *Centaurea macrocephala*, the great golden knapweed is a big, bold plant with strong stems each bearing a huge yellow flower. Although it is not the most refined of plants, it is immensely useful for rougher areas, perfectly capable of going it alone. Humming-bird hawk moths just love it.

The primary reason for growing vegetables is to eat them, but so many are such outstandingly

OPPOSITE
This picture is a reminder of just how lucky I am to be meeting these magical flowers and making these little films with such lovely people. The photographer's not bad either.

beautiful plants they are worth including in any garden just for their handsome good looks. Two of the most statuesque of perennial plants, the globe artichoke and the cardoon are also mouth-watering vegetables. They are very closely related – twins just about – and they share the same stature and appearance.

The majority of vegetables are annuals, completing their life cycle in one year, but there are a few perennial plants that provide food year after year – including sea kale, rhubarb, Jerusalem artichokes and the two forms of *Cynara cardunculus*, the globe artichoke and the cardoon. In the spring their jagged, grey leaves assert themselves through the middle of the desiccated clump of last year's plant. Within a matter of weeks they have made a couple of feet, and they continue to grow throughout the summer, making a magnificent show and providing real drama in the veg patch – or the flower border.

It is the bases of the stems of the cardoon that are eaten when they are young. In artichokes it is the flowers we eat. Actually it is the calyx of the flowers that is the edible part. Artichokes are thistles, and as such the fine filaments that form the flower are encased in

a series of overlapping sepals. The flowerheads are severed before the flowers show and can be cooked in several ways. It is the base of each sepal, thick and fleshy that can be dipped in butter and pulled off with the teeth, or when really young the small chokes can be stewed in olive oil and white wine.

Although artichokes are perennial it is best to renew them every three years otherwise they can become woody and unproductive. The best way to do this is to take offsets from existing plants in March or April. Fresh basal shoots on the outside of the plant should be detached by sliding a sharp knife between the offset and the plant and severing it below ground with roots already attached. These can be planted in fresh ground enriched with lots of good muck. They always look a bit sad to begin with, but with a good watering they soon perk up. If there is a permanent site for globe artichokes, and no possibility of creating a new one, it is best to remove a third of the oldest plants each year and grow an annual crop of vegetables or flowers before planting fresh offsets the next year. In this way the ground has a rest from the artichokes. For most people it is unlikely there will be room for more than three plants anyway so this is a straightforward operation. Most of us would not even have room for a separate artichoke bed but a plant or two could be included in any flower border. They're big plants offering a small crop, but the flavour justifies their extravagant square footage, and in any case they make such magnificent plants how could you not grow them?

OPPOSITE
Surely cardoons and
artichokes are the most
magnificent thistles.

Grasses

Grasses are one of the biggest genera in the world. They penetrate practically every corner of the globe. There are more than a hundred thousand species, each one of them specifically adapted to its environment. They are one of the most successful of all plant families, covering a fifth of the world's land surface. They are tenacious and versatile. Mankind's history and development is closely bound up with them – we eat their seeds as grain, cereal crops are the most important staple foods and our animals graze on them. It was only with the cultivation of cereals and the development of pasture that mankind settled, so at one level grasses form the very roots of our civilisations. In our islands grasses have played a hugely important role, not only in providing our daily bread, but in supporting the animals we keep.

One of the traditional practices here was that of cultivating hay meadows, cut at the height of their growth, dried and stored to provide winter fodder for livestock. The main component in those meadows, alongside wild flowers and herbs, were grasses. Not the Italian ryegrass cut for sileage, which is the predominant 'grassy' field now, but a rich and diverse mixture which was no doubt delicious – for a cow.

There are still remnants of these meadows – we visited one on the outskirts of Lady Farm in Somerset. We filmed on a morning in late September, the meadow drenched in dew with a billion tiny rainbows shimmering in the low sun. Its beauty was spellbinding. Most of the grasses and wild flowers were in seed by then, but a quick collection yielded a host of different species, a few we could identify but many we could not – each one was different and distinctive. The whole scene was set by a soft meadow grass, spread far and wide across the field, the epitome of daintiness and delicacy. Later the wind blew gently through the meadow and the garden beyond. Grasses have a special relationship with the wind; not only does it carry their pollen but it disperses their seed too.

Even if you've never experienced it yourself, probably the most evocative image of childhood is a meadow full of wild flowers and grasses. It is a romantic picture, and one few of our children are ever likely to enjoy. Intensive agriculture, concentrating on food production post-World

OPPOSITE AND ABOVE
Grasses are ubiquitous. Wherever you travel they are always close by. They are surely one of the most highly evolved of plant families, different species adapting themselves to a range of habitats from damp meadow to pure sand.

War Two, coupled with massive use of herbicides has all but done away with the meadow. The loss in habitat for invertebrates, birds and small mammals has been massive. Our native plants are the hub of the eco-system of our islands, and since they are diminishing so fast, gardens take on special significance in its future.

Cultivated cousins

Grasses are a familiar picture in many British gardens, most usually in the shape of a lawn, though in recent years using them ornamentally has become increasingly popular. Grasses have been grown decoratively for more than a century. Both Gertrude Jekyll, famed for her herbaceous planting, and William Robinson, the father of 'wild gardening', used grasses as an important constituent in their repertoires. Nonetheless planting grasses in today's gardens often causes consternation – should they be relegated to a 'grass bed' or contained in pots and arranged in a safe and staid way? The prairie planting aesthetic demands a large arena where swathes of grasses and perennials can intermingle and create an informal, almost accidental, picture – as though the plants had somehow arranged themselves. In extensive areas, especially in municipal planting, this can create a relaxed atmosphere and has the added advantage over formal bedding schemes of being wildlife friendly and easier to maintain. It has less relevance in small private gardens, but the feeling it creates can be emulated even in a tiny space.

First and foremost choose grasses that will love the soil, situation and climate in your garden. If your soil is heavy and wet, *Molinia caerulea*, the blue moor grass, will thrive. What a magical group of grasses they are, their two different personae emphasising the season. First they're green, blue and purple, sometimes with dark stems, joining in with the late-summer kaleidoscope provided by phloxes, sanguisorba and the first of the rudbeckia. Later they become golden and glowing in the autumn light, in close harmony with the russets and reds that abound in that season. They're balanced by clouds of asters, Michaelmas daisies, in soft blues, lavender and purple.

As you would expect from a moor grass, molinias prefer to grow in an open position where they can make their soft, rustling poetry, blown this way and that. There are few height limitations in anyone's garden, and most of the group are light and airy, providing see-through features rather than bringing the view to a halt. If you need something upright try *M. caerulea* subsp. *caerulea* 'Moorhexe', 'Moorwitch' or *M. caerulea* subsp. *caerulea* 'Edith Dudszus'. The sub-species arundinaceae provides the biggest

OPPOSITE
Given that all grasses have blades for leaves and inflorescences and seedheads of a very similar nature, they are remarkably varied.
TOP LEFT
Pennisetum alopecuroides 'Hameln', valued for its soft purple foxtails.

TOP RIGHT
Hakonechloa macra 'Aureola', elegant and striking – it hails from Japan, and it shows.
OPPOSITE BELOW
Stipa tenuissima. Quite the waftiest grass around.

group of these grasses to grow in our gardens. A personal favourite is *M. caerulea* subsp. *arundinacea* 'Transparent', and though this is a big grass it has a diaphanous presence and other perennial plants can be grown right up to its skirts.

For those on light, sandy or chalky soils, pennisetum is a better option. They lack the stature of molinia or miscanthus, but make up for it with a wealth of detail close to, where their fascinating bottle-brush flowers can be enjoyed to the full. For those gardening on dry soil in a sunny, well-drained site, especially in the southern counties of the British Isles, *Pennisetum orientale* will feel completely at home. It makes a dense clump, erupting with purple-pink bottlebrush flowers from July for months. Grow it where the sun can ripen its blades, at the edge of a border, beside a path or in gravel. It's wonderful with purple penstemons and dainty orange kniphofias. Gardening in colder, wetter conditions, *Pennisetum villosum* would be a better bet.

Many of the new pennisetum cultivars, and selections of *Pennisetum alopecuroides*, have been developed in Holland and Germany. One of the best, and the most amusing (humour in the garden is very undervalued), is *P. alopecuroides* 'Herbstzauber' – its multiple fluffy heads look like many furry caterpillars wondering where to go next now they have reached the top of their slender stems.

North-American *Panicum virgatum*, the switch grass of the prairies, adds a different emphasis, with twinkling inflorescence adorning its upright stems. From 1-2m (40in-7ft) tall, it is sometimes sea-green and blue, sometimes crimson and red.

It is then too that the mighty miscanthus family comes into its own. Some are huge but others, though still having great presence, are refined enough to fit in any garden. *M. sinensis* 'Kleine Silberspinne' or 'Kleine Fontäne' are both ideal, although our favourite here at Glebe Cottage is 'Flamingo'. Just as it sounds, it brings real panache to the early autumn scene.

Grasses add a new dimension – they shimmer and scintillate, sway and whisper, and bring movement and music into the garden.

Many grasses can be grown from seed, started either in the autumn when it is harvested or in the following spring. Sow seed thinly on the surface of loam-based seed compost (although any decent compost will do). Separate plants and pot individually when they have a few blades (if you leave it too long before pricking out there will be a dense mat impossible to separate). Seedlings of cultivars will not necessarily come true, but they are usually similar to their parents. If you want clones, exact replicas, then vegetative propagation (division) is the only way – as with all grasses that should wait till spring.

OPPOSITE
Molinias are some of the most useful grasses around, bringing to the garden all the qualities that grasses epitomise: light, sound and movement. *Molinia caerulea* subsp. *caerulea* 'Edith Dudszus' at its glorious, golden best.

WINTER WONDERS

When the last leaves fall from the trees, there is a tendency to feel down. And when crisp late-autumn days are replaced by spells of bitter weather, rain turning to sleet or hail, a feeling of despondency begins to get a grip. The knowledge that it's going to get worse before it gets better is difficult to take. And when a cold northerly wind starts to bite and you find yourself turning up your collar, it's tempting to think that it's time to head indoors.

Yet, just like every season, winter has its own special qualities, its own intrinsic beauty. Winter is stark, but that means that secrets hidden at the height of summer's glory are now revealed.

Shape, structure and texture can be studied now, appreciated in a way that would have been impossible when branches were masked by leaves, vistas obscured by the plentitude of summer's exuberance. The silhouettes of branches make ever-changing patterns. Twigs glitter with a thousand droplets, each one a glinting spectrum emitting its own tiny light.

Evergreens come into their own, hollies, lone signposts in the wood or along the hedgerow, can be seen in all their majesty – the king of the wood, the ruler of the winter. Female trees are laden with a rich, red harvest and ivy, in flower as winter begins, shines more and more brilliantly, those same flowers changing gradually to spheres of black berries. Redwings and fieldfares move in and the woods are full of the outraged squawks of blackbirds and the rustle of leaves as they vigorously dig and delve.

Far from being in a state of suspended animation, the garden is moving fast, though most of its activity is subterranean. Nature is at its most earthy now, and there is a dynamism in it that is just as powerful as that of spring. The noise of shoots retracting, stems withering, leaves falling has a deep under-rhythm as roots, tubers and bulbs begin to draw down strength and energy into the dark, rich soil.

The first shoots of snowdrops push through in wood and ditch, and in our gardens they are accompanied by hellebores, keen to take advantage of the lack of competition. Our wild hellebores, *foetidus* and *viridis*, get on with their quiet resurrection and before too long they're joined by the unscrolling leaves of Lords and Ladies.

There may be setbacks – deep snow, hard frosts, flood and tempest – but nature takes them in her stride and there, one day, as the sun breaks through, are the first celandines.

Arum

Plants that make their mark as winter bites are few and far between. Taking a country walk at the woodland's edge or along hedge-bound lanes, as the grass browns and disintegrates, and bracken holds its rusty sway, you may become aware of tightly scrolled buds thrusting upwards amongst the detritus of the failing year in complete contrast to the debris around them. Come back a week or two later and the leaves may have shaken themselves free of one another and still be ambitiously expanding, now green and glossy, marked with purple splodges, fresh and new – unstoppable.

As spring sets in its flowers take advantage of warmer weather, showing themselves gradually, again at first tight-scrolled, then bit by bit opening into broad spathes and rising from them an upright, perfectly erect spadix.

Enter the wild arum, *Arum maculatum*. It is a plant steeped in folklore, with a plethora of common names, most of them alluding to the sexual connotations which are difficult to ignore when you are confronted by it. It is cuckoo pint, (pronounced to rhyme with mint, pint here short for pintle – a penis) and the cuckoo more to do with cuckolding than to do with the appearance of the bird, Lords and Ladies, Jack-in-the-pulpit, willy lily – some commentators reckon there are going on for 100 common names for it.

The phallic spadix has at its base, deeply buried inside the spathe, the flowers. It's pollinated by insects that are attracted by its foetid smell and lured into the deep spathe, sometimes never to re-emerge. Both male and female 'flowers' ring the spadix, female flowers at the base and males above them. Long after pollination, after a quiet summer when no one pays any attention to it, the flower stem extends, pushing close-packed green fruits ever higher. Gradually they change to vivid orange, polished and alluring. Though they are poisonous to human beings, they are manna to hungry birds who devour them greedily and distribute them far and wide. The big white seeds contained within the pulp of the berries are either wiped from their beaks or pass through their dietary tracts and are expelled. In both cases they seem to germinate readily.

All arums seem to have contractile roots that pull the rootstock down deep into the earth. At one time these roots were used, dried and powdered, to produce starch and to make a drink – think I'll give it a miss.

Despite all the ribaldry surrounding its appearance, cuckoo pint is a quiet but handsome plant. It often comes up in the wilder places in the garden at Glebe Cottage. I am loathe to banish it, and in any case since the root stock multiplies so fast it would be well-nigh impossible to get rid of every bit.

OPPOSITE
Such simplicity and purity of form, *Arum maculatum* is a beguiling presence at the woodland's edge.

A. italicum subsp. *italicum* 'Marmoratum' is a close relation to our native arum. It is difficult to know whether to begin with the leaves or the berries when describing it. They are occasionally seen in each other's company, but the overlap is so fleeting that the plant has two distinct personae. The berries push aside the papery wrapping of the old flower in September to become the brightest thing in the autumn garden. Over the next two or three months, they change from glistening green through warm yellow and orange to their ultimate fiery red, clustering around strong stems like long-handled torches.

The first tightly scrolled leaves appear just as the berries vanish. They look a little incongruous, so new and strident while all around is mellowing and sinking back into the ground. This is just the beginning of the performance as one glossy-green arrowhead follows another, from winter into spring, unfurling to reveal ivory ribs and veins.

They seem impervious to even the most dreadful weather.

In established clumps the leaves vary in size, the larger ones coming from the main plant and the smaller from new side tubers, which *A. italicum* produces in common with many aroids. The most majestic leaves, from the most mature tubers, have particularly pronounced markings and sensuous, undulating edges. These render the pale-green spathes, produced by most plants in the spring, all but invisible.

Cultivated cousins

A. italicum subsp. *italicum* 'Marmoratum' is widespread over southern Europe and the Canary Islands, and has been cultivated here for well over three centuries, thriving in sun or dappled shade. Our best plants grow in deep fertile soil, but clumps flourish in all sorts of out-of-the-way places, courtesy of the blackbirds. Occasionally they take root on tree stumps or even in the hollows of living trees. Rather annoyingly, and in common with so many gatecrashers, they have the knack of making my planting look contrived.

It is easy to produce new plants without any help from blackbirds. Collect the berries in autumn when they start to fall away from the stems, and squeeze them to separate the seeds from the pulp. Push the seeds into the surface of soil-based seed compost, cover with a fine layer of compost and top with coarse grit. For faster results, lift an established clump, remove some of the bigger side tubers and replant them in the new site.

OPPOSITE TOP LEFT
Dracunculus vulgaris has an air of darkness and danger with a smell to match. Don't plant it near your kitchen door.
TOP RIGHT
Arum creticum is pure class. Dark, glossy arrowhead leaves make the perfect foil for simple elegant spathes in pure lemon. It needs cosseting.
OPPOSITE BELOW
Arum italicum subsp. *italicum* 'Marmoratum' gets on with it without any help.

Iris

Why include irises in the wintry section of this book? Surely they are in their full glory during the summer months? But there are irises doing their thing in every season, and one of our two native irises is at its most alluring during the winter months. *Iris foetidissima* has none of the glamour of most irises. They are grown for their appealing flowers, very often lavish and showy, not so *I. foetidissima*. Its flowers are shy and subtle, soft brownish-lilac, with a network of fine markings over the petals' surface. They are very beautiful but subtle, seldom noticed, flowering at a time when the garden is at its most flamboyant.

But, during the winter months *I. foetidissima* comes into its own. Amongst the shiny, evergreen, sword-like leaves the three compartments of the seedhead begin to open. The trio of capsules split apart like pea pods revealing glossy orange seeds which last right through the winter. *I. foetidissima* can still be seen growing wild. You may come across it in

Devon or Dorset where it is still hanging on, and there are colonies in East Anglia too. Its vernacular name of Gladdon or Gladwyn is derived from the Latin *gladiolus* – little sword.

Iris pseudacorus, the yellow flag, is our other native iris. Ubiquitous and easily recognised, it frequents waterways, ponds, lakes, streams and marshes throughout the British Isles. In our gardens it is usually represented by its variegated form, *I. pseudacorus* 'Variegata', its strong upright swords splashed with cream. It is one of late spring's brightest stars. Though it can be grown as a marginal with its roots submerged, it is just as happy dwelling in damp, heavy soil. Botanists believe that before the last Ice Age it was probably a landlubber, but it evolved rapidly to cope with wetter conditions as the ice melted.

Plants with vertical leaves are an essential element to provide ladders for aquatic larvae to climb when they are ready to transform themselves into their airborn incarnation. They are a vital element not only in nature but for any constructed pond, no irises or rushes, no dragonflies or damsel flies, no watching them transfixed, as they perform their glorious aerobatic displays.

OPPOSITE
The spherical orange seeds of *Iris foetidissima* burst from their casings as winter takes hold, many of them persisting right through the coldest months.

ABOVE
Yellow flag, *Iris pseudacorus*, one of the most widespread of our native flowers, thriving anywhere as long as it's damp.

Iris was the Greek goddess of the rainbow, fitting then that this family of plants should take its name from her since its colour range covers the whole kaleidoscope, from yellow to indigo. Not only is the scope of the iris family's colour comprehensive, but the plants provide their exquisite flowers in just about every month of the year. There are members of iridaceae for every sort of situation but the majority, whether their preference is for dry or damp conditions, love a sunny position.

Most members of the iris family and their relatives share common characteristics. One is that their flower parts are in threes or multiples of three. A classic iris demonstrates this graphically with three standards, the upright petals that encompass all the sexual workings of the flower, and three falls, usually the most decorative part of the flower evolved to attract the attention of pollinating insects and lure them in. They are often helped in this task by bewitching perfume. Iridaceae are monocotyledons with straight leaves with parallel veins that run from the base of each leaf to its tip. At the seedling stage all have single seed leaves, as opposed to the twin leaves of dicots, the great majority of plants.

Cultivated cousins

Irises themselves start the show as early as January. Every year in the garden at Glebe Cottage, come snow or tempest, the breathtaking flowers of *Iris* 'Katharine Hodgkin' appear in the first few weeks of the year. Their colouring is almost other-worldly, or sub-aquatic, with greeny-grey mixed with marine blue, strikingly marked with darker blue lines on the falls (no doubt to guide insects in towards precious pollen). The closely related *I. danfordiae* is next, just as short of stature – only a few inches tall but this time in vivid citric yellow. It got its name from an intrepid English lady, Mrs Danford, who purportedly smuggled some of its bulbs in her hat.

Reticulata and histrioides irises are the next to appear in gorgeous jewel shades of sapphire and amethyst. All these early irises are bulbous and the best time to buy them and plant them is in September. They are cheap enough, though certainly in the garden here 'Katharine Hodgkin' is the only one to keep flowering reliably year after year. The others tend to disintegrate and change to 'rice', the name given to the scores of tiny bulbs produced. The best advice to keep them in flower is to plant them deep, if possible with 15cm (6in) of soil above the top of their bulbs. I describe in my book *Grow Your own Garden* what to do if they do turn to 'rice'.

So-called English irises and Dutch irises are next on the scene. They are bulbous too, but much taller and more difficult to incorporate, partly due to their formal bearing but also because when they flower in April their

Through debris and detritus, sometimes even through snow, *Iris* 'Katharine Hodgkin' pushes up its pointed buds to reveal the most exquisite of flowers. Rusty oak leaves and *Arum italicum* make the perfect partners.

herbaceous companions have hardly broken cover. Some gardeners prefer to grow them for cut flowers in the vegetable garden. Their sumptuous colours, from blues and whites through yellows, purples and rich browns are especially cherished so early in the year.

May and June bring a smorgasbord of colour, frills and flounces as the voluptuous forms of the Germanic or bearded irises take over. It is unusual to find a flower whose colour range includes pinks and crimsons, blues, yellows and oranges and every subtle nuance in between. Often there are showstopping combinations of contrasting colour, and each year at the Chelsea Flower Show nurseries such as Kelways, Claire Austin and several French nurseries (Cadeux is one of the best) exhibit new varieties. It is fascinating to watch preparations – because irises are such ephemeral flowers it takes real skill and understanding to display them at their best. Each flower is individually wrapped in cotton wool or tissue and carefully unravelled at just the right moment so its petals unfurl for the judges and the first of the public to see the show. In cold years a very different procedure takes place employing hairdryers!

This group of irises has fascinated some of the most creative gardeners. Monet grew masses at Giverny, and was always on the lookout for new varieties, and they are still grown there where they relish the conditions – hot sun in the summer and free-draining alkaline soil. Several of Van Gogh's last paintings are of irises growing in the garden of the asylum at Saint-Rémy where he stayed shortly before his death.

The great plantsman E. A. Bowles grew beds of them in his garden at Myddelton House. They probably look at their best planted together, for again they are difficult to amalgamate with other plants – their show, although spectacular, is short-lived and their big, ground-hugging rhizomes need plenty of space to bake in the sun if they are to make a real show. They are not demanding plants – they thrive on neglect, preferring poor soil, preferably alkaline, needing little in the way of water or nutrients.

For the most part my garden cannot offer germanic irises a happy home (it is far too wet – they like it dry, but it is heavy clay) as they love free drainage. In the few places where we can provide hospitality, *Iris* 'Rajah' takes pride of place in vivid chrome-yellow and contrasting velvety maroon. Its plush petals are ephemeral, but it is so sumptuous – who cares how long it lasts. In Northern France they are grown on the roofs of cottages and another iris, *I. tectorum*, decorates roofs in Szechuan in China.

OPPOSITE
The showiest irises must be the bearded or Germanic irises. Upward-facing standards and tumbling falls in kaleidoscopic colours, often with the added attraction of sweet scent – all means to luring in insects.
TOP LEFT
Iris 'Rajah'.

TOP RIGHT
Clumps of iris quickly become congested. To maintain performance, dig them up, split them and replant, discarding the old, tired rhizomes.
BELOW LEFT
Iris 'Langport Wren'.
BELOW RIGHT
Iris 'Jane Phillips'.

In contrast many species need damp conditions. Butterfly iris is the common name for *I. ensata*, from Japan. During July their tight, pointed buds open to some of the most gorgeous flowers of the family. Many are single coloured and have classic form with broad, spreading falls held almost horizontally. But their popularity, especially in the USA, has resulted in extensive hybridisation and the production of many named cultivars, some of them unhappily with exaggerated flower shapes and decorated petals. There are gardeners who adore these big, showy flowers but I'm not one of them.

During later summer other iridaceae take over. There are dieramas, angel's fishing rods, with their long, gracefully arching stems decorated with elegant flowers in pinks, white and purple. As dierama flowers turn to seed and their stem tips almost touch the ground, the gladiolus clan step into the limelight. Again there are so many selections and cultivars to suit every taste. Traditionally many of the big, blowsy cultivars were grown in rows for cutting, and it's easy to overlook that within this branch of the family are some of the daintiest, prettiest and most unusual flowers imaginable. There are dainty 'butterfly' gladioli such as 'The Bride' – no prizes for guessing what colour she is – or 'Nymph' in pretty pink with teardrop markings. Perhaps my all-time favourite is *Gladiolus papilio* Purpureoauratus Group. It's not quite dingy in colouring, but quiet and soft purplish-grey with blodges of yellow, outlined in purple on the lower petals like the marks on butterflies' wings. Its colour has much in common with that of *Iris foetidissima*.

The last of the gladiolus to flower is *Gladiolus murielae*, formerly known as *Acidanthera murielae*, hailing from Ethiopia. Its upright bearing, coupled with gracious white flowers centred with deep purple and a rich, unexpected scent, make this a cherished plant. It is especially valuable for its late flowering, often through till the end of October. When temperatures drop lift its corms and store them frost-free through the winter.

To round off the year, in mild spells the tightly scrolled buds of the Algerian iris, *Iris unguicularis*, open in a day, expanding into classic form and bringing splashes of colour and exquisite scent to the winter garden.

OPPOSITE
Iris laevigata 'Variegata' in John Massey's garden. Even when the brilliance of the flowers has faded the white striped foliage will carry on the show for months.

Clematis

Anyone out for a country walk as autumn merges into winter is liable to come face to face with what is surely our most charismatic native climber. It has as many names as there are counties, and the great majority of them celebrate not its flowers, but its seedheads. One of its most common names is Traveller's Joy, a reference to the way in which it scrambles and ambles through hedges, up trees and over banks, adorning its hosts with lusty vines, green and vigorous in early summer, concentrating on expanding its empire. Later it opens its delicate, cream-coloured blossom, which eventually transforms into the characteristic fluffy seedheads. At first these seedheads are silken and soft, reflecting light so they shine and shimmer. As they age they become fluffier, more anarchic and more visible as the leaves on the branches and vines they adorn shrivel and fall.

Clematis vitalba is our only native clematis. It is steeped in lore – a plant both of the devil ('old man', from its common name old man's beard, is a pseudonym for the devil), because it is powerful, strong and strangles without a second thought, and yet deeply associated with the Virgin Mary, perhaps from the innocence and delicacy of its flowers and their sweet scent. Virgin's bower and lady's bower are just two of its names. Its stems were smoked in lieu of tobacco – apparently they burn steadily – and for this quality it has earned the name of lad's bacca or shepherds' bacca.

In common with other members of ranunculaceae it has no petals. The sepals of its flowers form spherical buds, protecting the boss of dainty stamens within until the right moment. They open in the sun of late summer/ early autumn, offering nectar to all-comers. It loves to have its thick, thong-like roots in the shade, preferably in alkaline soil with plenty of woodsy earth into which to delve, but it needs the warmth of direct sun to open its flowers fully. All clematis thrive in such conditions.

Cultivated cousins

There are a few plant species that give us flowers throughout the year, but to find one that does so with a seemingly infinite variety of colour and form is totally unexpected. The clematis family are all-rounders, there is something here to satisfy every taste and to fit in with every situation.

Although the vast majority are climbers or scramblers, there are herbaceous varieties too, which have their own ebullient charm but die back to nothing each winter only to start the performance all over again when spring starts to shoot. Of all these, *Clematis recta* 'Purpurea' has a special place. Its clouds of small, creamy flowers would be reason enough to grow it, but unusually its foliage is the main attraction.

OPPOSITE
Clematis vitalba, having run out of suitable hosts up which to climb, makes its way across the ground, smothered in a froth of its dainty, creamy flowers. They have a light and delicate fragrance.

Deep-purple, divided leaves clothe its strong stems from the word go, creating dark and interesting clouds along the border. They are a perfect foil for summer flowers and a thing of beauty in their own right. The colour of its foliage being so intense, this was always one of the most asked-for plants on our nursery.

By the time herbaceous clematis begin their spring season, *C. macropetala* has already opened its frilly lanterns of blue, pink or white alongside *C. alpina*. *C. armandii* has just come to the end of its deliciously scented flowering, and the fat buds of the indefatigable *C. montana* are bursting day after day.

This is just the start of the cavalcade. Soon, in June and July, *C. viticella* in all its myriad forms adds its magic to the mix. Its flowers are daintier, more elegant than those of the large-flowered hybrids, and have few of the problems (such as clematis wilt) that beset their overbred brethren. For the programme we were lucky enough to meet Richard and Yvonne Hodson in their garden, Hawthornes, near Ormskirk in Lancashire. They have one of the national collections of clematis, and the viticellas are Richard's main love. The way he grows them, and the imaginative ways in which he displays them, show his understanding of just what the plant is, what it needs and how it grows. He grows them through shrubs, up trees, obelisks and arches and in pots. There are no walls or fences in the garden, the traditional sites for supporting clematis, but Richard demonstrates that they are unnecessary.

Cultivars such as *C*. 'Étoile Violette' and 'Étoile Rose' have the multiple benefits of long flowering (often right through the summer), disease resistance and imperviousness to weather. As their name suggests, these have starry flowers. In complete contrast the flowers of *C*. 'Minuet' look like so many fairies' hats, bell-like with reflexed edges. A great advantage of using viticella cultivars on an arch is that they can be cut to within 30cm (1ft) of the ground.

The show-offs of the bunch, with voluptuous, stop-you-in-your-track flowers, are the large-flowered hybrids. They don't do grace and daintiness, but they do provide one of the most spectacular shows of the season. Some are fully double, and their colour range is phenomenal. Choose from hundreds of cultivars, some even developed to grow only a few feet tall for container cultivation. Even more striking, but with a classy charisma, *C*. 'Hybrida Sieboldii' is a one-off with creamy sepals and a flurry of purple petalloid sepals in the centre.

OPPOSITE
A collection of clematis, guaranteed to bring colour and grace into the garden from spring to late autumn.
TOP LEFT
Clematis macropetala 'Florilia', a spring flowerer.
TOP RIGHT
Clematis montana 'Elizabeth', smothered in flowers.

BELOW LEFT
Clematis 'Huldine' in the garden here.
BELOW RIGHT
Not content with flowering early, *Clematis* 'Bill MacKenzie' flowers again, its thick yellow sepals accompanying the silky seedheads from its first flowers.

Holly

'Of all the trees that are in the wood, the holly bears the crown.'

Holly is a magic tree, long revered as the protector and the bringer of hope. All evergreens were once valued as providing a living link between one year and the next, positive proof that the drear, bleak cold of winter would not last forever, that despite death all around, nature's life-blood still ran through the holly's veins.

Though holly boughs were brought indoors to decorate homes long before Christmas was celebrated in our islands, to cut down a holly tree to the ground was to invite bad luck. The holly tree was often used as a signpost, a reference point – even now when hedges have been flailed to bits, the holly trees that stand intermittently along their length are left.

Hollies not only helped and protected human beings, but offered (and still do) protection to sapling trees, which in many cases outgrow their former protector. It is common to find a holly tree growing branch in branch with an oak, a beech or a hawthorn.

In pagan myth the year was ruled by two kings. The Oak King, at the height of his power at midsummer, was constantly battling with the Holly King, who ruled the winter and whose power only started to decline after the Winter Solstice as each day the hours of daylight gradually grew longer.

Most evergreens come into their own during the winter. They are easier to see without competition from the leaves of deciduous trees and shrubs, but the best of them – the hollies – tend to be the also-rans of the horticultural world.

Why do we gardeners wait until Christmas before we give hollies a thought? They are amongst the most tolerant and accommodating of trees. Sounds dull? Faint praise perhaps? Not a bit of it. Hollies have everything going for them. Some have steely grey trunks, others have purple stems. Some are laden with berries in vivid red, or occasionally yellow or ivory.

They have lustrous leaves that retain their handsome gloss all year round. Their foliage can

OPPOSITE AND ABOVE
My favourite holly tree, a big, old *Ilex aquifolium* that the dogs and I walk past most days, though I always have to stand and stare. Close up you can really see what a munificent tree it is, packed with its glistening red berries.

be neatly margined in cream or splashed wildly in bright yellow. In some cultivars the whole tree is lit up by a golden or milky glow on the leaf surface.

Cultivated cousins

For those of us who prefer our leaves plain, there is the whole gamut of green, as rich and various as a close-toned Turkish rug (but not nearly so soft!). Some are desirable for their petrol-blue colouring, dense and dark with a mysterious air. *Ilex × meserveae* Blue Angel is recommended frequently by those in the know. Blue Prince and Blue Princess are similar. If you want berries too, choose the latter but make sure there's a male around.

Most gardeners' incentive for growing hollies is for their berries. A beautiful female tree adorned with clusters of red berries is hard to beat in the winter garden. But it takes two. Most hollies are unisexual, the flowers of each tree are single sex, so pollen must be carried from the male tree to the female, usually by insects, to produce fruit. Males can be marginalised, grown on the boundary out of sight, required only for their sexual prowess and function. Alternatively they can be included in the heart of the garden for their own sake and in their own right.

If you want to ensure a good set of berries make sure to have at least one male cultivar around to pollinate the females. That's not always as straightforward as it sounds since there are a number of hollies with inappropriate cross-dressing names. *Ilex aquifolium* 'Silver Queen' is a male, admittedly a very handsome male, with dark-green, glossy leaves slightly marbled in paler green and strikingly edged in ivory-white. Another impressive male plant, *I. aquifolium* 'Golden Queen', has broad yellow margins. Don't expect any berries if these are the only hollies you plant. But if nearby you add a plant of *I. × altaclerensis* 'Golden King', with broad, smooth golden-edged leaves, there should be berries galore. 'Golden King' is in fact a queen as she's female.

Ilex aquifolium 'Argentea Marginata' is the name of a group of hollies including both male and female plants. All are striking trees, and one cultivar, *I. aquifolium* 'Argentea Marginata Pendula', is a beautiful weeping tree with white edges to its leaves. It's a female so its long elegant branches can be covered in red berries – this is an excellent tree for a small garden. *Ilex* 'Silver Sentinel' or 'Belgica Aurea' has narrow cream-margined leaves and a slender shape.

Not everyone approves of variegated leaves, though, and for the purists there are any number of cultivars with polished, dark-green leaves. A female tree often recommended for reliably producing a heavy crop of sealing-wax red berries is *I. aquifolium* 'J.C. van Tol'.

OPPOSITE
Hollies and snow go together.
TOP LEFT
Covered in snow, an anonymous holly in a garden.

TOP RIGHT
Frost rimes the leaves of *Ilex aquifolium* and its accompanying yew.
OPPOSITE BELOW
Ilex aquifolium 'J.C. van Tol', renowned for its berries, gets the frost treatment.

To accompany them, there are dark, shiny leaves with smooth edges. But the tree has its detractors. Some find it a rangy grower inclined to stick out an elbow or two in an unbecoming fashion. *I. aquifolium* 'Golden van Tol' has the same faults and virtues, but its leaves are margined in gold.

Top marks go to *I. aquifolium* 'Pyramidalis', another cultivar of our indigenous species which, together with *I. aquifolium* 'J.C. van Tol', was awarded an Award of Garden Merit by the RHS in 1969. It belongs to the heterophylla group, which means its leaves are of more than one kind – some are spiny while others have smoother edges. It is self-fertile and reliably produces a heavy crop of berries. As its name suggests, it makes a good conical shape, and in maturity it becomes broader (don't we all). *I. aquifolium* 'Pyramidalis Fructu Luteo' is very similar except it has bright yellow fruit. The great advantage of any yellow-berrying tree or shrub is that the birds leave yellow fruit or berries till last, so gardeners can enjoy it throughout the winter. Another good yellow-berried holly is *I. aquifolium* 'Bacciflava'.

If, on the other hand, you can do without leaves during the winter, and want only the berries, forms of *I. verticillata* are deciduous and by the time winter comes they become just a mass of berries on bare stems. Unlike our native holly, *I. aquifolium*, which grows well on most soils and doesn't mind wet and heavy ground, *I. verticillata* prefers drier conditions and consequently does best on the east side of the country.

Whether or not it snows, a fine crop of berries on your holly makes the season more festive, and the birds will get their treat too. At Christmas time, references to holly and ivy are inevitable. Along with mistletoe, they are the plants of the season. We decorate our homes with them and use images of them on cards. Out in the garden their importance is much longer term, both for us and for the wildlife that frequents our gardens. Both holly and ivy are native plants, though most of our garden examples are cultivars and selections with 'special' qualities.

It's not just humans who have a soft spot for holly and ivy – this evergreen duo are two of the most important indigenous plants, both in the wild and, by extension, in our gardens, for wildlife. Perhaps the most obviously useful feature of the pair is the bright red berries of the holly. If you have ever been thwarted in your attempts to gather berry-rich holly by finding its branches stripped bare, then you'll know only too well how much birds enjoy the bright-red berries. After all, that's why berries are as bright and juicy as they are. The maturing of the seed coincides with the ripening of the berries

OPPOSITE
Variation can lend hollies a new twist.
TOP LEFT
The glossy green leaves of *Ilex aquifolium* 'Wateriana' are edged in gold.

TOP RIGHT
Its foliage splashed in yellow and bright green, *I. × altaclarensis* 'Lawsoniana' also produces a crop of brilliant berries.
OPPOSITE BELOW
Hedgehog holly, *I. aquifolium* 'Ferox', is always good fun.

and the time when hungry birds are actively searching for food. On a scale of delectability, red berries are top-of-the-tree. As we know to our cost, birds find berries a real treat. Packed with sugars and protein, they are devoured by resident blackbirds and thrushes, as well as flocks of visiting redwings and fieldfares.

Where there are berries there must have been flowers, and holly trees start to blossom in winter and early spring in most cases. Most trees bear flowers of only one sex, so to produce berries both male and female trees must be present. The flowers are tiny, well-hidden amongst the prickly leaves, but both male and female flowers produce nectar, ambrosia for early insects. There are few on the wing at this time of year, but attracting them is essential so a bargain is struck – insects get to eat and precious pollen is transferred. This is a wonderful bonus for wildlife when food is at a premium. Holly flowers are particularly important to holly blue butterflies, who raise their early brood on them. Equally important to this species are ivy flowers, as the second generation's caterpillars feed on them.

Holly is a noble tree but if space is limited it will happily live its life as part of a hedge. Hedge trimming must be fairly relaxed, though, if there are still to be flowers and berries. Holly is a versatile plant. Some species and cultivars make excellent hedging whilst other plants are destined for a solo part or perhaps a duet. Hollies as specimen trees can be magnificent, but they must be chosen carefully. They withstand pollution well and are unperturbed by traffic fumes or salt-laden gales.

OPPOSITE
Once upon a time, I used to make these holly wreaths for market. Now it's just for us.
ABOVE
Laden with their rich crop, female trees of *Ilex aquifolium* will provide food for countless birds throughout the winter.

Snowdrops

The nation's favourite flower is the rose, but if in the bleak days of winter you asked the gardening public which flower filled them with hope, for sure the snowdrop would win hands down. Nothing else can lift the spirits so surely as the vision of a bank of snowdrops, be they growing wild or carefully cultivated.

Even one brave new shoot pushing its way up through the daunting mire is enough to guarantee the succession of spring from winter. Day after day new shoots join in until there are crowds and crowds (never hordes or armies – snowdrops are far too genteel for that).

You seldom see a lone snowdrop. They are social plants, and we always talk about snowdrops 'carpeting' the woodland floor. Although they are fascinating at close quarters, it is en masse that they shine. The snowdrop that creates sheets of glistening white is also the most straightforward – *Galanthus nivalis*. *Galanthus* means 'with milk-white flowers', and *nivalis* 'of the snow'. Although nobody

is quite sure when the common snowdrop was introduced to the British Isles, it is such a familiar sight in gardens, hedgerows and woods it might as well be native. It loves shade in the summer and humus-rich conditions, revelling in loam and leaf mould. It relishes heavy clay where clumps get thicker year-by-year, spreading both by seed and by the bulbs dividing spontaneously.

At first sight snowdrops seem like an impossibility of engineering design – how can something so slender be so strong? How can this hair-fine stem, the pedicel, support the big white drop? No matter how thrashing the wind, the flower is free to dangle undamaged. The three pure-white outer petals shelter three inner petals, which form an underskirt tipped with green. Inside the secret workings of the flower, stigma and stamens, are protected. No matter how brutal the wind, or how heavy their swelling ovaries, they dance blithely, unfazed by weather. When they push up through snow they treat it as protection. The temperature inside the flower is two degrees warmer than the ambient temperature, protecting the pollen from damaging frost.

OPPOSITE AND ABOVE
Galanthus nivalis, our beloved snowdrop. There may be weeks between its first shoots breaking through and the white bells dangling from their fine stems, but every day its progress seems to mark a step closer to spring.

Later, when seed is set, the weight of the capsules brings them gently to the ground. Gradually they will open, dispersing their seed. The plant goes to sleep, grass grows around it and the summer cavalcade takes over. The snowdrops sleep until the earliest hours of the next new year, when they stir once more and prepare to announce the coming of spring. In the bleak midwinter, when gloom descends on most gardeners and enthusiasm is at a low ebb, to see grey-green shoots unexpectedly pushing through the sleeping earth is all it takes to cheer us.

Everyone can grow snowdrops. No matter how tiny your garden, nor how full it is of other plants, there is always room for a few bulbs. If you prepare their future homes thoroughly, snowdrops, once planted, will multiply and colonise, and each year you can look forward to a bigger and better performance.

The most familiar snowdrop is *Galanthus nivalis*. It is a woodlander, frequenting damp ditches, dingley dells, cool gullies, hedgerows and woodland walks. It appreciates humus-rich soil and loves deep leaf mould. If you have heavy soil, both snowdrops and narcissi will be perfectly at home and should increase well. A site in heavy soil, amongst the roots of deciduous trees or shrubs, suits them perfectly.

Not everyone has the luxury of space for a separate spring or woodland garden, but even one tree can provide a perfect setting for clumps of snowdrops planted through drifts of later-performing shade-lovers. You don't even need a tree. If space is at a premium plant your bulbs amongst big clumps of perennials. In the winter, when herbaceous plants are cut down, the snowdrops can be viewed clearly and appreciated fully. In the summer the perennials lend cool shelter to the now-dormant snowdrops. Both appreciate a good moisture-retaining mulch. Snowdrops will colonise quickly of their own volition, both by seed in the case of the common snowdrop and some of the selections from it, but also by their bulbs dividing spontaneously.

Although they signify the coming of winter's end for British gardeners, nobody is quite sure whether or not they are native plants. Snowdrops have little regard for boundaries. They cover thickets and woods throughout the United Kingdom as though they'd always been here. They have a close association with man, often naturalising themselves close to habitation. Old neglected gardens and churchyards have proved to be amongst the most fruitful sites for discovering 'new' snowdrops.

Cultivated cousins

Snowdrops have never been the subject of hybridisation, but new forms with bigger flowers, different markings or quirky shapes crop up from time to time. They are always seized upon by ardent galanthophiles (snowdrop obsessionals).

Almost all galanthus have the familiar white nodding flowers, hanging on a hair-fine stem with a white petticoat edged with green. Occasionally the petticoat becomes a tutu, with layer upon layer of inner petals. The double form of *G. nivalis*, 'Flore Pleno', has just such a flower. Because these double flowers are sterile, they flower for a long time so are particularly valuable in a small space (although they cannot produce seed).

There are a few small clumps of special snowdrops in one of the herbaceous beds here at Glebe Cottage. These treasures, some of them gifts from generous snowdrop connoisseur friends, others snapped up at shows and plant sales, are mollycoddled in the hope that they will increase. In other parts of the 'shady garden', each bed has just one variety of snowdrop, combining with different groups of pulmonarias and hellebores and every year or two we divide the snowdrops and replant so there are now substantial carpets of white under the bare trees.

There is *Galanthus* 'Atkinsii', very early, large yet elegant with big flared bells. *G.* 'S. Arnott' has colonised one small bed around some of our best yellow hellebores. Apart from the wild *G. nivalis*, *G.* 'S. Arnott' has a very special place

in my affections – most snowdrops have a delicate scent but the fragrance of *G.* 'S. Arnott' is exceptional. Its large, rounded white bells have a glorious honeyed perfume. It is a winner in every way – one of the best for all-round garden value with a compact yet graceful form. It is trouble free and seems to increase well. From a few bulbs bought ten years ago we now have several small drifts. As soon as the groups begin to get crowded they are lifted and divided (when the flowers begin to look tatty) – they're replanted individually about 10–15cm (4–6in) deep. Fresh compost and leaf mould are worked into the new site before planting.

Snowdrops have their own mythology and their own special place in our culture. Joe Sharman, a galanthophile extraordinaire, knows the stories and fantasies that surround each and every snowdrop. He is intrigued by the history and ethnobotany of snowdrops, and has probably the most extensive collection of snowdrop memorabilia anywhere. He tells me that during Victorian times they were a symbol for hope and purity, there was even a Snowdrop

OPPOSITE TOP AND
BELOW LEFT
Galanthus 'Atkinsii', one of the first and most elegant of snowdrops, eventually becoming quite tall.
BELOW RIGHT
A double form of *Galanthus nivalis* 'Flore Pleno' having a race with *Eranthis hyemalis*.

League for Young Ladies, and snowdrops were a 'logo' on the labels of bottled mineral water.

Because of their seeming indestructibility they were often planted on graves (cemeteries and graveyards are a prime venue for galanthophiles searching out new snowdrops), and gradually their public persona became more and more closely associated with darker concerns. They appeared on funeral cards, and by the beginning of the First World War their image had become synonymous with sadness and death. They lost much of their popularity.

Times change and now they are once more in favour, enjoying an even greater popularity than they did during the Victorian era.

Unlike most bulbous plants, snowdrops are not planted as dry bulbs. Because they grow away so early they have already made new roots, embryonic shoots and flower buds while other bulbs, like daffodils and tulips, are still dormant. Planting dry snowdrop bulbs is seldom satisfactory. Often they have been stored for long periods of time and are totally dormant, and they usually stay that way, never bothering to wake up. Planting 'in the green', when the plants are in growth, gives them the chance to settle in. Roots are already growing and as the flowers and leaves wither, their goodness travels back to swell the bulbs which will rest throughout the summer in readiness for next year's show.

Dividing snowdrops is important to maintain vigour (and increase numbers), but there are two schools of thought on this. Traditionally the optimum time to replant is 'in the green', as the flowers fizzle and the foliage dies down. But there is another school of thought that they should be moved when they are dormant, as long as they are not allowed to dry out. John Grimshaw, one of the leading authorities on snowdrops and ex-Garden Director at Colesbourne Park (which houses one of the most extensive collections of snowdrops in the country) is part of the latter school.

Whether you already have snowdrops, you're lucky enough to have generous friends who can donate a clump or two or you've bought them mail order from a reputable grower, the best time to transplant them is as they finish flowering. Shake the soil from the bulbs and replant individually a few inches apart and 10–15cm (4–6in) deep. Give each bulb a ration of good humusy compost, preferably mixed with leaf-mould. Vary distances between the bulbs to ensure a random, natural look. Within a short space of time, big drifts can be created.

OPPOSITE
Even *Galanthus nivalis* 'Flore Plena', the double form of our wild snowdrop, sometimes makes substantial colonies. Here with a mossy log – the perfect backdrop.

Hellebores

Meeting a new flower 'at home' is an unmitigated thrill. Throughout the series, we visited and filmed with more than 20 of the wild flowers you've been reading about in this book. In many instances I had been lucky enough to make their acquaintance earlier, in fact many of them are neighbours of ours frequenting the woods and hedgerows around our cottage while some were old friends from my childhood. It was with great excitement though, that on our first expedition I prepared to meet *Helleborus viridis*, one of our two native hellebores. We had become acquainted before, but the *H. viridis* I met then was cultivated, sitting on a sales table at an RHS show, masterfully grown and beautifully presented by Alan Street on the Avon Bulbs stand.

In fact our relationship had gone further, money changed hands and the said *H. viridis* travelled home to Glebe Cottage. It seemed happy for a while but sadly had a reverse of fortunes and went into terminal decline.

Alan had told me about seeing this dainty green hellebore growing in rough grass in Gloucestershire, and I had yearned to see it for myself.

On a brisk, bright February day we came face to face in a wood close to Ware. We had already found *H. foetidus* earlier in the day, and visited Fiona Harrower to see her magnificent collection of *H. × hybridus*. By the time we reached the wood the afternoon was waning. When I write 'we came face to face', it has to be understood that such intimacy could only be achieved by my lying down beside it.

The green hellebore is a dainty, not to say diminutive, plant, doing its thing before the rest of the carpeting plants at the woodland edge are up and about. You could see nettles just beginning to leaf up between the little colonies of the hellebore, and imagine that later in the year they would grow up far taller. They'd protect the hellebores while they set and distribute their seed, giving them extra shade later in the year.

ABOVE
Helleborus foetidus, our biggest, boldest native hellebore, though it still has rather a subtle, quiet persona.
OPPOSITE
Helleborus viridis, truly shy and retiring, though bees and other pollinating insects early on the wing must track it down for its valuable pollen and nectar.

Our meeting was all I'd hoped for and more. The sepals are a pure, opaque springtime green, and the flowers perfect chalices, gently hanging their heads, with the characteristic collection of gold-dusted anthers at their centres. The foliage, dark and deeply divided, surrounded each little group of flowers. This small community must have been there for some years, many of the plants sowing themselves into the mounds of naturally composted garden waste and building rubble that had been dumped at the edge of the wood. The underlying soil was alkaline, full of flints – just the sort of conditions that hellebores seem to love.

Our first encounter earlier that day was with *H. viridis'* big brother, *H. foetidus*. It is again a native plant that loves poor conditions and alkaline soil, and it's at its best on limestone pavements, which is where I first encountered it with my mum and Neil. It was a memorable day. The year after my dad died, we'd gone up to Morecambe Bay to see the waders who mass there in their millions, and later we travelled up into the hinterland of that beautiful part of the world. There were huge colonies of

H. foetidus growing on the limestone, their deeply-divided leaden foliage giving them a dramatic air. Most plants boasted several sturdy stems, each bearing bunches of globose lime-green bells edged with crimson. You could detect the aroma that gives it one of its common names – stinking hellebore. It's supposed to have a meaty smell but I confess, though I'm a vegetarian, the smell is not abhorrent – quite pleasant in fact. No doubt it has evolved to ensure that any insect around will be drawn to it and aid pollination. And here it was growing in the scrub at the woodland's edge as it had probably grown for many thousands of years.

Cultivated cousins

Over the past decade the popularity of *H. × hybridus* has rocketed. All the rage in Victorian gardens as an embellishment to the shrubbery, the Lenten Rose gradually fell out of fashion. Only in the second half of the twentieth century did interest pick up. It accelerated at such a pace that now most gardeners would recognise one at first sight, and many of us regard them as an essential ingredient in our garden menu.

Were hellebores to flower in midsummer they might not get a second look, but coming at a time when all around is bleak and bare they win our attention then our adoration. The fact their heads hang down adds to their charm – it is not until you turn each one upwards that you appreciate the enormous diversity of colour and pattern that each plant contains – all different. This is one of the treats of spring. When I had a hip replaced in February several years ago, my

OPPOSITE
Pollinating your own hellebores is easy and rewarding.
TOP LEFT
Taking pollen from the anthers of the 'father plant'.
TOP RIGHT
The seedpod, marked with embroidery thread, swells.

BELOW LEFT
The seed capsules burst, revealing the shiny black seeds.
BELOW RIGHT
Seed is collected into brown paper bags.

major frustration as I was recovering was that I couldn't bend far enough to see my hellebores. I toyed with the idea of mounting small mirrors on the end of my crutches.

The flowers hang their heads to protect their precious pollen from destruction by violent wind and rain – after all, these are flowers which are at their height when the weather is at its most deplorable. A plant that braves such inhospitable conditions must earn our respect, but it also earns our thanks for giving such a display and transforming our gardens at a time of little hope and very limited expectations.

A further attraction is that hellebores are easy-going plants, which fit in with the modern gardening ethos. They lend themselves to naturalistic schemes and informal plantings. Not only are they easy to place, they are also easy to grow – providing conditions are right, their successful cultivation needs no special skills, and anyone can propagate them from seed.

Gardening isn't just a question of finding the right plants and putting them in a spot that suits them. As in nature, it is the companionship and interrelation between plants that turns a collection into something beautiful and remarkable.

Hellebores are amongst the most undemanding, yet the most beautiful of winter stars, making an effect from January, through February and into March and beyond. Part of the reason they look so good for so long is that their petals are sepals. Once flowers have been pollinated, instead of falling off, as do the petals of most flowers, they persist. Whatever their

original colour they eventually become green, at which time they fit in with any other plant, but their colours, even in full bloom, are subtle and easily associated with other flowers and foliage.

It is the relationship with other plants that makes or marrs the pictures we create. In midsummer there are countless plants at the pinnacle of their performance – choices are endless. In late winter and early spring, there is a more limited vocabulary. Juxtaposition of colour, texture and form need consideration – and imagination. The overall scene is far starker. We need our plants to work well – together.

Hellebores love a bit of shade and humus-rich soil that doesn't dry out the same sort of conditions enjoyed by so many other woodlanders. One of the classic combinations is to surround clumps of hellebores with pulmonarias. Yellow-flowered forms of *H. × hybridus* (orientalis as was) glow more brightly next to vivid blue pulmonarias. The best of all the deep-blue cultivars is *Pulmonaria* 'Blue Ensign' with unusually large flowers and rich-

OPPOSITE TOP LEFT
Tightly curled buds are protected by caulescent leaves.
TOP RIGHT
An exceptional *Helleborus × hybridus* with dark nectaries and the nuance of a picotee edge.
OPPOSITE BELOW
The shady part of the garden at Glebe Cottage is thick with hellebores.

green leaves, slightly crimson on their reverse. Our own indigenous hellebore, *H. foetidus*, looks lovely rising from clumps of *P.* 'Opal'.

The old *P. officinalis* 'Bowles's Blue', now known as *P. officinalis* 'Blue Mist', makes fine, upright clumps. Surround it with some of the low-growing evergreen ferns – *Polystichum setiferum* with finely cut lacy fronds, or *Polypodium vulgare* for a more solid, upright effect. These ferns contrast wonderfully with big clumps of any of the more brightly coloured hellebores, or the pure white forms. This combination makes a clean and simple duo, or the two can be combined with clumps of *Arum italicum* 'Pictum'. Closely related to our own cuckoo pint (or Lords and Ladies), this European plant has the added attraction of distinctive white midribs and veins on its prominent, arrow-shaped leaves. Winter and spring are its seasons and it looks equally well with snowdrops as with hellebores – in fact all three often overlap.

Many bulbs are ideal companions to hellebores. Many of the dark-flowered hellebore selections and cultivars arrive early in the season, and their intense, saturated colour is underlined when they are planted amongst sheets of white snowdrops. Eranthis, winter aconites, provide glowing basal colour around hellebores, the bright-yellow flowers with their green ruffs adding detail and an extra layer of interest.

Many of the blue bulbs, chionodoxa and scilla, are perfect partners and can be encouraged to naturalise by allowing seedheads to form and scatter their seed willy-nilly. It only takes a couple of years for seedlings to flower.

We tend to grow our hellebores in small beds surrounded by gravel paths, and limit the colours within each bed. This is the easy way out, but it does make their impact stronger. In one bed, for example, there are coral-flowered *Pulmonaria saccharata* with strongly spotted foliage, bold meandering clumps of *Ophiopogon planiscapus* 'Nigrescens' and a series of apricot-pink hellebores. In between, clumps of my favourite, dead nettle, *Lamium orvala*, push through their scarlet-backed shoots adding an air of mystery to the vernal proceedings.

Further up the garden several large clumps of *Astelia nervosa*, their silvery swords lit up by the thin winter sun, used to form the best of all backdrops for clumps of dark hellebores. Intermingled with early narcissi and clumps of *Leucojum aestivum*, the so-called summer snowflake, it was the sort of picture that stayed in your mind all year round. The astelias died in the last harsh winter, but they were part of such an unforgettable picture we're going to try and recreate it again.

OPPOSITE
When *Helleborus* × *hybridus* are happy they make big, healthy clumps, loaded with flower. This one seems happy.

Celandines

The celandine has to be the smiliest plant ever – one flash of sun and its buds open into wide, starry flowers with polished petals. No petals in the world are as yellow or as lustrous as those of a celandine. Buttercups come close, after all they are near cousins, but the shine of celandine flowers as they open wide in the first spring sunshine is almost dazzling. It is joyous.

Ranunculus ficaria is the earliest of the buttercup clan, and the first flowers often show themselves before the end of February. It has evolved to cope with torrential rain by closing its petals (really sepals) to protect its inner workings when skies darken. Its petals, or sepals, are green-backed, camouflaged until the sun re-emerges.

Like so many spring woodland flowers it is a 'Cinderella plant', accomplishing its whole cycle above ground in a matter of months. It flowers, is pollinated, sets and distributes seed by the time the clock strikes twelve and the canopy fills in overhead. It is a creature of hedgerows and damp banks, with beautifully marked leaves accompanying a bounty of golden flowers. Despite the disappearance of much of its former habitat, it is still relatively common in our countryside thanks to a tremendously successful root system and the production of masses of seed, which germinates easily and quickly. It is this ease of proliferation that makes it anathema to many gardeners. Its roots are composed of a collection of tiny rhizomes joined together in one crown in an unusual construction – this prompts its common name of pilewort. Every little rhizome is capable of developing into a fully fledged plant and this happens rapidly.

Under the medieval Doctrine of Signatures, celandines were used as a cure for piles – a sort of pre-homeopathy. Whatever its medical efficacy in curing physical woes, there is no doubt that psychologically it fulfills an important function – the sight of its polished golden flowers (and that means the sun is shining too) is enough to banish the winter blues and make us all feel better. Its common name, celandine, comes from *cheladon*, the Greek for swallow. Though the flower arrives long before the bird, the arrival of both is a declaration that spring is on its way. Other country names include golden guineas, and bouton d'or.

What do you suppose was Wordsworth's favourite flower? Daffodils surely? Well no, in fact the flower he worshipped above all others was the humble lesser celandine – *Ranunculus ficaria*. He wanted to be associated with it when he died, but unfortunately they got it wrong and it is an image of the greater celandine, *Chelidonium majus*, that decorates his monument. He wrote three poems to the lesser

OPPOSITE
Ranunculus ficaria, our native celandine, in full and complete control. There is no more joyous sight on a sunny spring day. No wonder this was Wordsworth's favourite flower.

celandine full of admiration for this plucky little plant which so early in the year braves the elements, and on the first sunny day after its emergence opens its dull buds wide and thrusts up its vivid-yellow stars with their polished petals, as forthright as any plant could be.

In the garden, attempts to weed it out are often counter-productive. Yet if it can be controlled it makes one of the best splashes of colour in the early garden, in full flow long before the majority of herbaceous plants have thought of getting out of bed.

Cultivated cousins

The straightforward wilding is beautiful, but there are many others, discovered in the wild and brought into cultivation by sharp-eyed botanists and gardeners. *R. ficaria* 'Brazen Hussy' is far-and-away the brightest and most cheerful of all the 'cultivated' celandines, with vivid-yellow flowers nestling amongst bronze leaves Found by Christopher Lloyd in the woods at Great Dixter, it has become a favourite for a spring show in damp ground. It is probably the best of the lot, and bright-blue spring skies are reflected in both its flowers and foliage on a sunny day.

There are a host of others from the neat, perfect rosettes of *R. ficaria* Flore Pleno Group, so symmetrical they look like an illustration from an Elizabethan Herbal, to the massed creamy petals and mucky bronze leaves of *R. ficaria* 'Double Mud'. Some people make collections of them – in addition to the flowers being so different in form, and sometimes in colour, the leaves vary too. But to my mind nothing can outshine the wilding.

Cautious gardeners will worry about bringing any celandine into the garden's hallowed ground – they are notorious self-seeders, and just one rhizome broken from the central clump of roots will happily grow into a full-sized plant while your back is turned. Avoid this by planting celandines pot and all – as long as the rim of the pot is slightly below soil level they will never dry out. If you want to propagate it (it's child's play to pull the roots apart and repot) it is easy to dig up the pot and, if space is at a premium, replace it with a summer flowerer in late spring. Don't forget to deadhead your celandines if you don't want them to spread.

OPPOSITE TOP LEFT
A tapestry with *Ranunculus ficaria* 'Brazen Hussy' weaving itself here and there.

TOP RIGHT
A double celandine. There are numerous strange and unusual forms of celandine.

OPPOSITE BELOW
Rather than competing, these two invaders seem content to call a truce. *Crocosmia* and *Ranunculus ficaria* 'Brazen Hussy'.

Index

Note: page numbers in **bold** refer to information contained in captions.

Acknowledgements

Jonathan Buckley is the best; his love of wild flowers and of all plants shines out of all he does. His photographs go straight to the heart of the matter and reveal the souls of his subjects and their intrinsic beauty. He brings the reader into intimate contact with the plants he portrays. You feel you are there with them.

Working with Jonathan is always such a positive collaboration, he always strives to make everything as brilliant as can be and makes me feel that nothing but our very best will do. He has many other less celebrated talents too! If it weren't for his intrepid orienteering skills, not to mention the GPS app on his phone, we might still be wandering around the sandy wastes of Braunton Burrows. We were there on one of the hottest days of last summer, miles from civilization, Jonathan loaded with heavy equipment in the midst of seemingly endless dunes. Where's a camel when you need one? We had no water and discussed the efficacy of extracting moisture from marram grass – that mirage in the shimmering heat, was it Lawrence of Arabia or Ray Mears? We struggled onwards, or was it sideways, but thanks to Jonathan eventually found his car.

Once again it has been our good fortune to work with Lorna Russell, our commissioning editor. If it weren't for her sterling work and her total belief in us this book might never have been. Thank you Lorna for encouraging us, trusting us and making sure we have the space and freedom to do the best we can and at all times for nurturing us and this book and helping bring it into existence. Thanks to our project editor, Joe Cottington, for all his enterprise, hard work and his patience. Andrew Barron's design is a tour de force and shows our work in its best possible light. It is a huge privilege to work with him.

Both last year and this, our strand on *Gardeners' World* has taken us up and down the country visiting wondrous wild places and meeting their wild flowers. We have seen extraordinary gardens and met fascinating and remarkable people who have played a vital role, sharing not only their expertise but their enthusiasm. I'd love to mention them all. Hazel Bishop who introduced us to her garden and her pulmonaria, both called 'Cotton Cool' was typical. She was thrilled to share both with millions of viewers. Sadly she died recently.

The diligence, devotion and downright creativity of our crews has produced and, without doubt, will continue to produce some outstanding television. What an enormous privilege and what fun it has been to work with our delightful director Tom Weston, Rob Yeoman our researcher and our usual crew, captivating cameraman Gary 'the heron' Hawkey and the unruffled and sublime Stevie Beech as well as all the other crews we've worked with up and down the country. Our little films have been beautifully edited – thanks to all our editors and post-production people for turning them into something very special. I must not forget the peerless Paul Barnett, our director for the first programmes in 2012.

Thanks also to the girls – Jo Mainwaring, Trudi Cresser, Liz Rumbold, Louise Hampden, Gill Tierney and Alison Kirkham – for getting behind this project and making it work.

Thanks especially, and as always, to my inspiration – Neil, Annie and Alice.

Most of all thanks to the wild flowers – and their cultivated cousins – for being who they are and just for being there.